Praise for *Worth*

"It takes a lot to impress a jaded Vivian Blaxell I think: Wow! A multi-dimensionality of conscio... through gendered spheres of pleasure, strife, disappointment, hilarity. Always at the core of her personal is an empathetic participation in the plights of all species. Blaxell's blunt, elegant sentences are thoroughly modern, yet they exude a depth that speaks to previous centuries. I see her as a sort of 21st century Proust committed to TMI. "My vagina is not a good judge of character." This is what writing should look like. This is what writing should do."
— Dodie Bellamy, author of *Bee Reaved*

"This is an astonishing book — a complete, byzantine personality revealed by degrees in a whirlwind of associations, from the metaphysics of transubstantiation to the terminal shit. *Worthy of the Event* is a living thing, seductive and hypnotic, borne aloft by its rolling cadences."
— Lucy Sante, author of *I Heard Her Call My Name* and *Low Life*

"*Worthy of the Event* vibrates with becoming, a moving (not so) random walk into a life richly, bitchily lived, beauty and/in its disappearance, philosophy and literature, trans theory and theorists, variegated transphobias, fucking, empires colonial and nuclear, sex work, the joy of thinking and her disappointments, love. The most provoking writing I've read in so long, all that old transsexual shit, tremulously there and gone, a text blissfully here to go back to."
— Trish Salah, author of *Wanting in Arabic*

"Vivian Blaxell takes the events of her life and gives them a new event — this book. An extraordinary book for an extraordinary life. A book that's curious, expansive, erudite, generous, shapely. A book that gives the reader the enormous gift of knowing that we can all become worthy of what knocks the life into us."
— McKenzie Wark, author of *Love and Money, Sex and Death*

"In her seventies, Vivian Blaxell looks at life through the lens of transness, and transness through the lens of life, in a series of essays that defy all categories but one: they are events. Like that of her patron saint Gerturde Stein, Blaxell's prose is intimate, candid, bold, and erudite, as she explores a wide sweep of subjects—childhood and family, sex and love, being and becoming, culture and colonization, technology and catastrophe. She take us on joy rides that break the speed limit, run red lights, swerve between lanes, detour through worm holes, and by the time she's done sirens are going off everywhere."
– Diana Goetsch, author of *This Body I Wore: A Memoir*

"*Worthy of the Event* is a daring and radiant debut. Vivian Blaxell's prose is as bewitching as it is paradoxical: poetic and prickly, intimate and distant, singular and polyphonic. I adore how she tangles with topics, creating sharp and delicious connections across time and space, weaving details from her uncompromising life to create an intricate, organic, and alluring work that feels like a web, a nest, and a haute couture dress. This is a pulsing banger of a book."
– Hazel Jane Plante, author of *Any Other City*

"An electric, surprising, and revelatory use of the memoiristic essay form. Blaxell's passion for Life lifts off every page: by which I mean Life Itself, not just her own. Her pursuit of life in all places and times and her ever-hauntedness by the legacies of imperialism are integral to her work. Becoming, far more than being, is where Blaxell points, and I, for one, very much want to travel that way with her."
– Elisabeth Plumlee-Watson, Loganberry Books (Shaker Heights, OH).

Vivian Blaxell

Worthy of the Event

an essay

Copyright © 2025 by Vivian Blaxell

All rights reserved. No part of this book may be reproduced in any part by any means — graphic, electronic, or mechanical — without the prior written permission of the publisher, except by a reviewer, who may use brief excerpts in a review.

Published by LittlePuss Press, Brooklyn, NY
littlepuss.net

Cover design by David Knowles
Edited & typeset by Cat Fitzpatrick

MIX
Supporting responsible forestry
FSC® C008080

Earlier versions of "the diappointments" and "the disapearance of a.k.a. Victor Mature" appeared in *Overland Literary Journal*; an earlier version of "nuclear cats" appeared in *Meanjin*; an earlier version of "stardust" appeared as "La Folía" in *The Believer*.

ISBN 978-1-9643229-9-5 (print)
ISBN 978-1-9643229-8-8 (e-book)

1 3 5 7 9 10 8 6 4 2

> ...*self-enjoyment* is being worthy of an event, knowing how or managing to be worthy of the event... Whatever the event might be, be it a disaster or falling in love, there are people who are unworthy of what happens to them, even when these are not very prodigious events. Being worthy of what happens!
>
> – Gilles Deleuze, "Leibniz and the Baroque" Seminar, April 7, 1987

table of contents

I: the disappointments 9
II: mouse eats communion wafer 53
III: nuclear cats 89
IV: the disappearance of a.k.a. Victor Mature 125
V: indifferent to prayer 163
VI: stardust 200
VII: the practice 233

Worthy of the Event

I: the disappointments

My vagina disappoints me.

There, I've said it now.

Fairy says, "You think too much about where your vagina comes from," by which Fairy means *how* I got my vagina and not the *where* of it, not whether this vagina of mine hails from a place more exotic than a public hospital in a suburb of Sydney, Australia, with a view of a race-course from one side, the airport on the other and the burning plumes of an oil refinery wavering night and day in the distance. A vagina from Casablanca, maybe; I don't know. But the truth is, my vagina could be Made in Japan, straight out of the Audi factory at Ingolstadt, could be Louis Vuitton Vaginas of Paris, Vag by Dre, Pussy della Prada, an Apple vagina, I won't go on, but the point is this: this vagina of mine could have been bestowed upon me by celestial beings visiting from some sidereal, heavenly manna it could be, this vagina, a mote of paradise between my legs, yet, still, my vagina would disappoint me once a week or so. The rest of the time: okay.

"My vagina is not a good judge of character," Fairy says, and pleased about it, I can tell. We both need to be reminded that vaginas and vulvas are not agents, they are not even agentic. *I* need to remind myself that this vagina of mine can't do anything *to* me. I must take the blame for all my vaginally disappointed moments; I must stop speaking about this vagina as the cause of any disappointment. I must stop speaking of disappointment as an effect of this vagina of mine. But what is the right language for no blame? I am disappointed in or by this vagina?

No.

What about: I find this vagina of mine and the whole down-there apparatus disappointing (sometimes)?

Yes, that's it, there's no-blame-my-blameless-vagina in that, is there, but then Fairy says, "It's not your fault, Schatz," which may be the least Germanic thing ever to come out of Fairy's curlicue mouth. She, herself, refuses to let her vagina and her vulva off the hook. Fairy won't hold herself responsible for any of it, especially she will not be responsible for the libidinous desires and the disappointments she feels when she wants sex that she thinks she shouldn't want with people she shouldn't want sex with but does, me, for one example. "*She* wants what she wants. *She* can't get enough. *She* wants more and I cannot do anything about it," Fairy says.

Do vaginas and neovaginas have different ways of being and doing vagina then? Innocent vagina; vagina guilty? I want to say to Fairy, Is your vagina ever a he? But things between Fairy and me are already disappointing enough.

One doctor looks at what I've got and says, "Well, yes, this seems like a reasonably functional neovagina; however, I can see that your vulva might be a bit of a disappointment, but let's face it, that's the sort of vulva *etcetera* you got on the public health in 1972."

Dr. Eugene Schrang has made I-don't-know-how-many neovaginas and vulvas, not ten thousand, but a *lot* in Neenah, Wisconsin by the time I drive up there from Baltimore. He says, "It'll cost you thirty-seven-hundred dollars to improve the appearance of exterior things a little but at this point, all those revisions already, all that scarring, there is a limit, how old are you, are you sexually active, you might have to get used to a disappointing situation. Look on the upside: the rest of you is gorgeous."

I shut my thighs **bang** and say, "As long as you include decent pain management, three thousand seven hundred seems worth it. I'll write a check."

Dr. Ron Barr says on camera in 1983: Many psychiatrists who have been involved with transsexuals have come to be more cautious, and er, and er, er, er, er, more doubtful about reassignment surgery especially in view of the fact that the, ah, surgical results, are, er, often not very good, disappointing, and, er, it's difficult to know what to make of that but I suspect that this question of getting a functional vagina is a problem in different hospitals around the world.

Norma Mapagu says, "Stop watching that old video. There are better things to be disappointed about than vagina. Some people are disappointed with God, of all things. Why don't you try that?"

Worthy of the Event

✷

In seventeenth-century Amsterdam, Baruch Spinoza grew up under the sway of a Jewish God: God unitary, God the first and final cause of human existence, God intentional with a personality and a definite character. By the time of *Ethics*, though, Baruch Spinoza had refuted this Jewish God and been expelled from the synagogue to live as a Jewish excommunicant among Christians for whom God was one *and* three, the creator and cause, a personality, with character, a planner, a father, and template of the human form.

In *Ethics*, Spinoza proposes and describes a completely different kind of God to the God of Jews and the God of Christians, Catholic or Protestant. Spinoza's God is God-not-in-any-way-a-man. The *Ethics* version of God lacks a single human quality. This God is a kind of God *thing*. *It* does not speak. Spinoza's God does not have seven-day project plans. Spinoza's God is not even alive in the way human beings understand alive, not the Living God, but something entirely ineffable, and certainly never a celestial overlord planning every detail of life on the planet and beyond: the stone that falls from a cliff and kills a man, leaving his wife and children to starve, is not a part of God's great plan. Pancreatic cancer is not a part of God's plan. God did not send that asteroid, the sky falling into what we now call the Chicxulub crater near the Yucatán Peninsula in Mexico, as part of a Godly plan to end the dinosaurs. That lotto win has nothing to do with God. God help me, you might say in earnest, but help is not forthcoming or, if help comes, it comes not from God.

Sometimes I ask myself: from where did Spinoza's repudiation of the God character, God with a (big) personality, God the man with a plan come? Did the child, teenager, young man Baruch Spinoza experience some disappointment with the God of the rabbi and his God effects? Did that disappointment do as disappointments sometimes do, if we are lucky, go **boom**? Did some disappointment with the God of his fathers turn Baruch Spinoza into a philosophical rocket thundering away forever from immortal soul and The Law into an elliptical orbit around a black star where he found no God character, no God personality, no intentional God, no God role, but God `a being absolutely infinite, i.e., a substance consisting of an infinity of attributes and modes, of which each one expresses an eternal and infinite essence`, God the *universal* material?

To be honest, it was probably a good thing Spinoza was already dead when *Ethics* came out. The idea that humans are not images of God but just one of a zillion God modes triggered howling refutations. The States of Holland and West Friesland banned everything Spinoza had ever written and, even though Spinoza's inhuman, modal, haphazard, unspeaking God excited the likes of John Locke, David Hume, Gottfried Leibniz, and Immanuel Kant, *Ethics* had to be read and discussed in secret, for both synagogue and church saw heresy in it.

Worthy of the Event

Baruch Spinoza's God the substance with a zillion modes might have struck *me* at twelve or thirteen as a way out, that child I was, swotting up on what was called Bible Stories in that Seventh-Day Adventist school five mornings a week in that country town and withering every Sabbath Day under the threat of immolation or persecution or both: Behold, the Final Days approacheth. Spinoza's God the substance thing rather than the Father might have ended all those years listening so close to all that talk and singing about God's love, so vigilant for signs of my own progress toward the Second Coming, so intent upon finding a way for God the Father to love me enough to take me up to eternal life at the feet of Jesus Christ Our Savior in the New Jerusalem, all gold and pearl and precious stones. "Fucking boring, that will be," Julie Foch said as loudly as she dared.

I liked Julie Foch's big nose, let me kiss it, go *on*. Also, I worried about the proposition that all human beings are made in the image of God. I asked, and Pastor Bullock assured me I was, indeed "Made exactly in God's image, as are humans all, even that Wiradjuri mob living out by the city dump, can you believe that, they are in His image."

We had no pictures of God with which to check congruity or its opposite in the matter of how much in His image I and anybody really was, but there *were* pictures of Jesus Christ Our Savior and The Son of God, who, Pastor Bullock said, had been one hundred percent human, Jesus Christ and who, I assumed, as a human being must have been made in God's image. The picture we had of Jesus Christ had golden hair shining and eyes as blue as lapis lazuli. I had, what did I have, well, I *was* fair, but shining almost never happened, and as for the Son of God's blue eyes, The Aunts said, "Well, you look just like your mother, that mouth and those greeny hazelly swampy eyes, that's you your mother."

Being in the image of my mother was fine with me, but was my mother God, and if my mother was not God, which seemed very likely, and just another human being made in the image of God who was a man or at least in the *form* of a man as far as I knew, how could a man make a woman? Pastor Bullock said, "God the man crafted the first woman from the rib of the first man God made in his own manly image, so there's the explanation for that, get it. Also isn't it time for you to go home. Your poor mother must be awaiting."

I went home where there was not much God the man and no God the substance thing awaiting. At home, there was the man I called Him, and Him had trouble with me. "What the bloody hell are you?" Him said more than once a day. What a good question that was, but not a question to be answered unless I wanted a fist, which sometimes I did. "I am an angel," I said once, which brought a Him whack and falling black stars at noon. "I am a bird," I said another time. Him said, "You are a bloody galah, that's what *you* are, get out of the house and don't come back until your mother gets home from work."

"In your arse," I said or something similar learned from the Fischer boys.

Whack. "You blooming specimen. Get out, you will, and bloody well stay out." Whack.

Worthy of the Event

My sister said, "Stop it, oh, stop it," even as Him pushed me out the back door and latched it from within.

Over the fence the dog and I went and up the hill into the bush for hours. The dog panted and leaned on me and I became a piece of white quartz warmed by the sun, an ironbark with the wind talkative in my green and clattering hair, a single yellow furry pill of wattle blossom, the queen of all she surveys until my mother came home.

In the end Him died alone, his desperate lungs clogged by knobby reefs of cancer. He died spurning any and all pain medication because that is what a man is. He deserved what he got. Yet, to be accurate about Him, I have Him to thank for me giving up on Pastor Bullock's God, and, thanks to Him, I tacked toward life without authority, to life free of Gods with plans, to life without any kind of father Godly and ungodly, nothing. Since all was all nothing at all, I also felt nothing at all about that tall and narrow man in those black-and-white photographs with his neck arched in a way that showed a doleful soul. My mother made a point of telling me, "That's your dad, look: here's the one of him in his Trans Australia Airlines pilot uniform. Here's your father fishing for sand whiting off Bullroarer Beach. Here's your father laughing," but the whole your-father story, including the part about how my father's own mother cast his young ashes into the Tasman Sea where they vaporized into a racing cloud and reincarnated as rain for a kahikatea tree in Aotearoa New Zealand, was as unlikely, was as nothing to me as a trip to Jupiter or Dubrovnik. Heavenly daddy, dead daddy, daddy fucking mother in the bedroom, daddy throwing his dinner at the wall, daddy crying in the night, daddy of any kind, any type of heaven, any type of God, boring or riveting, Spinoza God, any eternity in any celestial city of bling, any *belief* coming with instructions became as the enemy to me. Thank you, Him, you brute.

"We never did see eye to eye," Him said and cough cough cough ten thousand miles away, forty years after.

"I was a child."

Thanks to Him, I became all nothing, all no. Even if I could have yessed, I would not have yessed. No to that Coleman Street Seventh-Day Adventist Church God who was not going to do much for me no matter how much I did for him. No to anything requiring any act of faith: your mother will come home in two weeks – no; Him will love you like a father now – no; this drought will end – no; Jesus wants to wash you clean of sin – no, no, no, no, no, no, no, no, no, not raging no, no, not even obstinate no, no, no to boy, no to I am not a boy, no to girl, no to I am not a girl, no to human, no to I am not a human, no to in-between, no to fixed and no, my mother is not my mother and father in the one person and no, I won't come home in time for dinner and no I won't stop looking at you like that, I will not surrender, I won't come to Jesus, I will not come to you, **no**.

"That face you've got on yourself these days, it's like you've fallen into the Slough of Despond sort of thing," my mother said.

I said, "Have you even read John Bunyan?"

My mother smoothed the back of one white glove and, while smoothing, she said, "That nasty tone, I hope you realize you are not dressed for church."

"I won't be going there again," I said, and said something like, "It's meaningless. No."

On that winter's day, my mother wore the little pillbox hat she had made of white rabbit fur and a lot of millinery buckram for shape and always tilted to the left for church and upon my "It is meaningless", she tilted her head too and said nothing except, in a considered way I had not yet seen in my mother, a drawn out, "We———lllll."

Then a considered silence and, "Ye———s, well."

Another consideration. "Yes."

"Yes."

"Well, then," she said and patted the rhinestone brooch done as glittering ears of wheat and drove her little white Toyota off into that pitiless white winter sunshine we got out there then.

I lay on the bed watching the white light turn the white slats of the venetian blinds to white fire. I drifted upon a white ocean of no and wondered how to get to the Bay Area, whatever Bay Area was, and the Summer of Love, whatever love was. Julie Foch had slipped me a dog-eared, contraband set of the Rider-Waite Tarot with a little white booklet of interpretations losing its staples and while my mother sang "Rescue the Perishing" from her pew at the Coleman Street Seventh-Day Adventist Church without me for the first time, her white lapin pillbox hat stiff and keeping the beat, I took The Tarot from its hiding place and, following the instructions in the little white booklet of interpretations losing its staples, I laid out a Celtic cross which seemed deliberately obtuse, except I did not yet know the word obtuse, and in it, I looked for ways to say yes, yes, yes; I examined the cards for how to surrender any disappointment with God and human being, to give up nothing and the worst of my no no nos and speed into an agreeable future where a yes for me would be revealed and I would be worthy of the revelation.

※

If God is not an über-human but a substance, as Baruch Spinoza shows, then heaven may not be a place, or, if heaven is a place, it is radically heterotopic, a place so different we can't recognize it as a place and, if we could recognize it as a place, we might be frightened by heaven or even bored to death, or just disappointed. It's not what they said it would be, we might whine. I expected more of heaven, how disappointing this place. We may gripe about heaven like any tourist let down by the slippage between the brochure, the web site, Instagram and IRL gripes and doesn't care for it, for is not disappointment with place forever and everywhere and always a risk, especially with famous places, places with a reputation for fabulous or beautiful or awe-inspiring or just fun, places we long to see or believe we *should* see.

They keep lists of places in Japan: the three most beautiful places, the three most beautiful views, the three best lakes, the three most beautiful beaches, three valleys, three waterfalls, islands, streets, historical sites and on and on, ten thousand lists but no list of the three best vaginas, neo or not. There is one Japanese list called Nihon no sandai gakkari tokoro:

Worthy of the Event

THE THREE GREAT DISAPPOINTING PLACES OF JAPAN
No. 1 – Sapporo Clock Tower, 1878
This place is an Important Cultural Property that doesn't seem important or even cultural if you're thinking Japanese culture. Perhaps foreigners find Sapporo Clock Tower charming, a bit of New Hampshire Live Free or Die architecture dropped in Japan and the building *was* exotic in its time, but many Japanese are just disappointed now even though they probably know the building is part of a grand story about Japan bringing modern civilization to the frigid wilds of Hokkaidō in Japan's own Age of Empires. Sapporo Clock Tower seems too small to be an important part of any vast tragedy, of any triumph of nineteenth-century modernity. Sapporo Clock Tower's clapboard walls, white, and its clock chiming the hours at the bottom of a thicket of office towers are too anodyne to express or even refer to Japanese destructions of Ainu First Nation society and culture using policies and techniques adapted from destruction of Native American civilizations in the western United States and Canada. If the weather is warm, many visitors give the place a beseeching glance then wander down the tree-lined boulevard or stalk off toward the distant grail of the shopping mall at Sapporo Station. In winter, which is often even colder than any New Hampshire winter, disappointed tourists grumble to each other, really very small, I can't see the point of that, and climb quickly back into a heated bus or car.
No. 2 – Kyoto Tower, 1964
Kyoto Tower's space needle design was meant to represent a giant Buddhist votive candle but ended up more The

Jetsons than the Dhammapada. It rises incongruous and 1960s-futuristic in the heart of a city any foreign visitor expects to ooze the kind of history that is free of any kind of futuristic anything except perhaps Miroku, the Buddha of the Future. International tourists pull faces and what the fuck is that as their bullet trains come into town, disappointing. But for me and a million others, Kyoto Tower is the kind of disappointment worth having. The outlandish arrangement of the white-and-orange concrete spire on its glass podium in the foreground, the great tiled roof of Higashi Honganji beyond, `a grey shale/ Mountain over the town`, and the pagoda eaves of Tōji further off up the slope of the eastern hills is a welcome-home sign, for, if you live in Kyoto, you get used to Kyoto Tower, even welcome it in the distance: almost home.

No. 3 – Harimaya Bridge, Kōchi, n.d.

Harimaya Bridge is disappointment itself, quintessence. Japanese tourists visit Harimaya Bridge just to experience the disappointment. Its official reason for existence is commemoration of a tawdry and disappointed romance between a monk vowed to celibacy and a young woman of the town but, in all its glossy spotless red and black tiny splendor, not a single trace of lower-case-r romantic can be found at Harimaya Bridge. The little tragedy upon which the place depends is missing and history is absent too, since the prohibited romance story is almost certainly apocryphal. `I have never been more disappointed` writes one Japanese contributor to Trip Advisor and appends an I-am-very-happy emoji.

Worthy of the Event

There are many there are perhaps millions of people who know by now that there does not have to be there. Gertrude Stein refuted the thereness of Oakland. She did not let it, not because she was disappointed with the place, but she did not let Oakland because Gertrude Stein the writer did not want Oakland to have the thereness necessary for disappointment to arise. She was probably aware directly, or via William James or somehow, of Niels Bohr's view of there, of the argument that entities have only probabilities until they are observed, at which point, probabilities become properties. Upon her immortal return to Oakland after many years away, Gertrude Stein refused to let Oakland be more than a probability. She erased the place she no longer knew: `Anyway what was the use of my having come from Oakland it was not natural to have come from there yes write about it if I like or anything if I like but not there, there is no there there,` and saying Oakland is not there made it not there. At least Japan's Three Great Disappointing Places list admits there is a there there at Sapporo Clock Tower, that there at Kyoto Tower is there, and even the ineluctably pathetic Harimaya Bridge has an undeniable thereness, thereness of a disappointing place being, of course, the prerequisite for any disappointment there provokes.

※

Colonialism striates, it gouges the places it takes with its own feelings about the business of taking the place, desire and I am going to fuck you in one way or another very often, but disappointment is also there. Disappointment attended empire. Mt. Disappointment is there in the Kulin Nation's traditional forest lands not far north of Melbourne, also called Naarm, that most livable city which can be a disappointing place if you are expecting livable to be like Vienna livable. Mt. Disappointment got its name, which is certainly not its true name, when a couple of British explorers of a place already completely explored and mapped by its rightful owners slogged to the summit expecting a grand panorama of New Holland, which would soon become Australia, all the way to the sea, only to find that old growth forest occluded any view. How disappointing.

Kumpupintil, in the Western Desert region of northwestern Australia, was called Lake Disappointment for more than a century after another explorer needed fresh water and found only a large salt pan. At Kumpupintil, you come up on the relationship of disappointment to power: the Martu people, to whom the land irrevocably belongs, never called Kumpupintil Lake Disappointment. They found the name affixed by the white man demeaning and destructive: the lake is the site of Martu creation and complex Dreaming in which the past, the present, the land, the mundane and the sidereal and who you are exist together. After a long political campaign, Martu elders convinced the government of the Australian state of Western Australia to remove Lake Disappointment from the maps forever and there, there is Kumpupintil which had never gone away. Not disappointing.

Worthy of the Event

The colony known as French Polynesia has the Îles du Désappointement, a group of small coral islands in the Tuamotos. The truly awful Fernão de Magalhães a.k.a Ferdinand Magellan called these islands Unfortunate because he could find no water there; bad luck, Magellan, but unfortunate is not necessarily disappointing. The Disappointment appellation comes from John Byron, another of those disappointed British explorers. He was not disappointed because no water but because the Polynesian people for whom the islands were home made it clear they did not intend to welcome him, get out, how disappointing for John Byron. Japan has tiny Gakkaritō (Disappointment Island) off the coast of Iwate Prefecture, which is land taken from its original people, Emishi, by the armies of Emperor Saga in the early ninth century

In the United States, there are Disappointment Peak in Wyoming, Cape Disappointment in Washington, and also a town in Oklahoma not disappointing but just Okay. *Death in Disappointment, Kentucky* is the title of one of Peter Ketchum's found monochrome photographs, over-dyed and marked with color and shadow. It appears to be an image of a young man being choked by a disembodied hand, erotic or homicidal, I don't know, but when I drove through the Disappointment Creek area on NK-11 on one of those sprightly autumn days you get in the western hills of Appalachia, it did not seem to be a place for any variety of strangulation, let alone disappointment. Another Disappointment Island lies in the subantarctic waters of the Southern Ocean, more than four hundred kilometers south of Aotearoa New Zealand. Ninety-five percent of all the world's white-capped albatrosses live here.

Albatrosses are the least disappointing of all living creatures. By wingspan, but not by weight, they are the largest animals in the sky under their own power. They fly high, they fly very far, they fly very fast. Albatrosses cruise on spread wings for hours and hours, barely needing to use their flight muscles. Albatrosses may stay aloft for days, avoid land for months, coming only to rest for short times on the surface of the sea and to breed. Unlike other birds that fly, albatrosses do not avoid storms; they seek the ocean squall, the typhoon, the cyclone, the El Niño hurricane. They fly into the shrieking turbulence. They mount the thunder and ride.

The white-capped albatrosses on Disappointment Island wander skies from the Tasman Sea and the Southern Ocean to the Indian Ocean and across the Pacific. "Vagrant" white-capped albatrosses may be seen hovering over ships in the South Atlantic Ocean and cruising the lapidary shores of Las Malvinas Falkland Islands from where they return upon the winds and clouds of storms to Aotearoa New Zealand waters and to Disappointment Island to reunite with their lifetime mates and make chicks. In their search for food, albatrosses use a mathematical fractal called Lévy flight: they patrol the seas and the shoreline in a pattern of long flight segments followed by short hops in random directions. This appears to be not instinctive but *deployed*. Albatrosses use a Lévy flight path to optimize foraging just as some human beings use Lévy path fractals to optimize bidding in online auctions, engineering procedures, data analysis, and financial decisions. If reincarnation is real; if Immanuel Kant is wrong to say the human soul signifies a substance only in the idea not in the reality, and if I may make a choice about the body into which my soul decants and reincarnates me, I might choose the storm rider body of a wandering albatross, and not just for the flying but for the albatrossian ability to stay away and be never disappointing.

When W starts calling me The Albatross and sends me beautiful watercolors of albatrosses and poems he has composed set down on the watercolor in handwriting so arabesque it is calligraphy, I take it as a Romantic-like-Shelley-or-Keats gesture. W sees nature in me, adores me as I flirt with cyclones and fly alone, I think, all dreamy, but it soon becomes clear that W's translucent washes of color and his serifs in ink encode a lower-case-r romance of another kind. He is working off *The Rime of the Ancient Mariner* or something.

"Are you a girl," W says when we first meet at that party and both of us about to have our eighteenth birthdays, and we spend the night together in the host's guest room because I am technically homeless, and W lives with his parents. When I undress and W realizes not that I am not a girl but that I am not the kind of girl he imagined me to be and then he realizes that me being not the kind of girl he imagined me to be is more troubling than he had figured it might be but he wants it still, he is disappointed, although not disappointed enough to go home and stop touching me everywhere, and then he is disappointed that he wants me as burning hot as he wants me, and I am disappointed that W is troubled by me, and disappointed, too, by my own disappointment which has a self-blaming edge to it. That's what you get.

This thing with W goes on in that disappointing, disappointed way for the next three years. W cannot stay away from me, and I cannot keep W away. He cannot be with me for too long without trouble, then disappointment. I cannot be with W too long before the no. W wants me to hide myself. Something about it causes disappointment in me or himself, who knows. "Put it away," he says, but I will not put it away no. What is the point of putting things away? Am I a kitchen cupboard, a toy box, a closet, a Westinghouse refrigerator? No. I am me.

Norma Mapagu says, "You with not put away is what W wants but he doesn't want to want what he wants."

This is too complicated for me, and even were it simple, I will not put it away until I am ready to put it away.

W is disappointed. He disappears but returns, inevitable, and we do it again, inevitable, and on we go like this, heaving in, rattling out, trying to find a steady rhythm, a decent breath in a brume of give it to me now and get out immediately, do not come back, I won't be back, please and no until the albatross poems and pictures start to show up in the mail, until I see W standing in the little street behind the Clock Hotel outside my home at three in the morning staring at the front door, until he hammers on the door raging at me, "I could kill you and even dead you'll drag me down," and I pour hot water on him from the upstairs window. In this disappointing affair W makes me into some upper-case-R Coleridgean-type albatross and himself into a born-in-Trieste version of the seaman who kills the albatross in a fit of rage and is then blighted by its death forever, and the story goes on and on and on until W meets someone who *is* disappointed or something by what she has between her legs and puts it away so that others may not be disappointed or something too, and then W goes to her and never returns, never says goodbye. There is no I am going from W. No I've found something less disappointing, something I can want without not wanting it. He is unworthy of the going event and only grabs me one last time, wrenches up my blouse and bites me seven times on my stomach and tiny garnets of blood jewel up around the marks left by his beautiful teeth.

"Rabies, darling, you will be frothing at the mouth and rolling your eyes about even a hint of water soon," Big Denise says and she dabs my wounds with a cotton ball soaked in Stolichnaya which she says is the usual instrument of moving on.

※

Edward J. Kempf was a psychiatrist at the St Elizabeth's Government Hospital for the Insane in Washington, D.C. He wrote charmingly in 1916 about humanoid cognition in the conduct of six macaques named, much less charmingly, A, B, C, D, E, and F – apparently the desire for food is stronger than the desire for sex among macaques – and also wrote, not at all charmingly, about two bisexual women with schizophrenia, who he also named according to the letters of the English alphabet; this man, Edward J. Kempf, devised the concept of homosexual panic, which has since been taken and bowdlerized by lawyers, police and court systems and killers to justify and excuse fists and boots, kicks and blows, knives and guns, strangling and beating and executions of gay men and especially, I understand, of women like me.

I was disappointed and then got real angry that she didn't tell me she was born a boy, US Marine Lance Corporal Joseph Scott Pemberton said after he strangled and then drowned Jennifer Laude, her beautiful face in the toilet bowl in a room in a motel in Olongapo, which is a port city about two hundred kilometers from Manila. I went into gay shock syndrome, Joseph Scott Pemberton told the court. His mother told the media that her son's sister is a lesbian so he wouldn't hurt any LGBT person, ever. The judge sort of agreed with something said or read and he downgraded the charge from murder to homicide, which were not the same things in the Philippine legal system. Joseph Scott Pemberton acted out of passion and obfuscation, the judge said in 2015.

The death penalty did not thus apply to the man who killed a woman because what he saw as her gender obfuscation disappointed *him* when, as Edward J. Kempf would have explained, it was Joseph Scott Pemberton's disappointment in *himself* for desiring Jennifer Laude that triggered his attack, his rancor, a kind of ressentiment of what she *had*, by which I do not mean *cock* but the knowing immanence that haloes every human being who throws their body against the cruel and false unnecessary binomial gender order that most of humanity has come to accept as natural despite all the scientific evidence to the contrary; *that* man was sentenced to ten years, and spent five of the ten in a Philippine military detention center, quite comfortable at Fort Aguinaldo, then, at the behest of the United States government, President Duterte issued a full and unconditional pardon, and Lance Corporal Pemberton flew home to Massachusetts in the middle of the 2020 SARS-COV2 pandemic.

Norma Mapagu says in a rush, "If Pemberton killed *you*, *your* beautiful white transsexual face would be dead in the plumeria-scented waters of a Toto Neorest Washlet with all the functions, including asshole blow-dry, in a suite at the Manila Okura and Pemberton would get a lot more trouble for killing a woman like you than the sort of trouble he got for killing a beautiful transsexual Filipino who was, you know, not really like you."

I say, "I *was* stabbed once, with intent."

Norma Mapagu says, "Show me the scar."

I say, "Show me yours."

But neither Norma Mapagu nor I want to show anything other than perfect.

Jennifer Laude's roommate says, America is still the favorite. And there is still discrimination. If Jennifer were a real girl, the conviction would automatically be murder.

✳

Some say that after I called my mother collect from a phone box outside a shuttered strip club in the morning and thin winter sunshine and gave her a précis of my current I-am-a girl story with tears added for both effect and supplication, my mother went into my childhood bedroom and locked the door for a day and a night. Nobody knows what she did in there. Anyway, my mother came out the next morning in time to do a lamb chop and fried tomatoes and toast and Maxwell House for Him's breakfast. She fed the birds in her garden. She smiled at shoots of very early lettuce and spoke kindly to the popping buds on her magnolia tree. She saw herself in the poppies flowered too soon and bound to get iced tonight. She went to the post office and sent me a greeting card with French bulldog puppies in sparkles on it, poste restante: `There is nothing wrong with you. I love you, you are my child, come home anytime. I'll make something nice for dinner` and something about lemons and lemonade. My sister likes to say our mother in my childhood bedroom that night cried for hours, so disappointed, but I don't think so. My mother knew *something* was to be expected out of me, she did. "You are nothing but **trouble**," she had said to me ten thousand times and sometimes whack whack, slap and slap again, but there was ever some tender part of my mother ajar to trouble done in bold and 14 point, to queers and sluts and people with demons and difficult kids, to me.

  My mother was disappointed about things other than me: impoverishment, husband dead young, Him, cold houses, bones crumbling to chalk, the price of eggs, her inability to shuck off some guilt about something obscure to me but as wrenching as an overdose of strychnine to my mother. Eventually all that disappointment flattened my mother. She turned into a two-dimensional woman, thin as a piece of paper, flat, flat, flatter, thin, a crude sketch of herself until she disappeared completely into the black star, bequeathing us a disconsolate estate of lesser disappointments, things given on birthdays, Mother's Day, Christmas and discarded, most completely unused, all stuffed to the dust-bunny back of a storage closet: three milliliters of Jean Patou Joy, Extrait de Parfum, the seal unbroken and still in its black box shining; two packs of Nioxin system for thinning hair never removed from the Christmas red wrapping; a strand of white Mikimoto pearls; two large tubes of L'Occitane Shea Butter hand cream; a burgundy and grey Princess Galitzine silk scarf; one Mexican handwoven cotton and alpaca throw blanket; a black cashmere cardigan with gold buttons in the knot pattern; six tubes of Mor hand or body cream; a huge Lao silk shawl in a rust and olive-green check pattern which I took back for myself, and one Arita porcelain bud vase from the Fukagawa kiln, its neck broken and repaired with superglue.

On a summer Wednesday afternoon when my neovagina was still very neo, my mother asked for a look. "Give me a squiz. I am your mother," she said.

I could not say no to that. My mother *was* my mother.

She looked at my still very neo and said, "That is rather."

I thought that *was* disappointing, wasn't it. I wanted more. Rather what? How does rather feel? Tell me how you feel about that, how that works. Has that changed anything? How is life with neovagina or what's the neovagina story? My mother never once asked: how disappointing.

Oh, don't you say it. I know I could have should have prompted my mother: don't you want to know, I could have should have said to her, just *ask*, ask me, please, but the chances of a big no from my mother, a know what, or why would I want to know about *that* were too high for me to risk the question even after three glasses of Riesling, and, honestly, I wanted unprompted. I wanted my mother to ask, what is it like, or even say, I *know* and I am sorry, tell me more, because my mother *did* know some of it, she had been told, but something stopped my mother from saying she knew and what she knew for all those years until her health failed and the black star neared, not yet full and opened above the river yet, only rustling in the shadows of the blue hydrangea hedges, but more there than not there, and it was only then that death and the next place on the horizon forced it out of my mother after curried sausages with too much salt. She stood up as if to orate and she said, "I know, I didn't, and I am very sorry, and you've made the most of it," and my mother clutched the edge of the sideboard with her right hand as though very sorry might whisk her away a bit sooner than she hoped. I looked at the right hand clutching and thought: talons, and I thought, `All mothers are guilty. All mothers are guilty.`

"How were the curried sausages," she said.

I said the curried sausages were too salty and something about childhood food being disappointing now.

Worthy of the Event

My mother said, "I suppose I didn't put enough love into it."

※

There are at least ten thousand disappointments, and ten thousand should be enough, *surely*, yet people keep on making new disappointments, gender disappointment, for example, which is not the gender disappointment of looking at your body in the mirror and seeing it's not the right body. Nor is gender disappointment the disappointment of being addressed as Ma'am and referred to as she when you are pretty sure it should be Sir and he. Gender disappointment is not the disappointment one might feel when the gender affirmation pathway of your choice has gone as far as you wanted it to go and your socials and your embodiment are now where you wanted them to be but where you wanted to be is not untroubled, not disappointment free, it's not a bed of roses. Gender disappointment is not that. Gender disappointment is not my mother retreating into a room for a day and a night upon getting the news about me, no. Gender disappointment is the disappointment that comes when the biological sex of a fetus identified by medical imaging fails to comply with the gender wishes of one or both parents who never seem to understand that these things will be decided in the future and in utero is not the future and in the futures of the fetus and mom and dad, gender is always up for grabs. When we found out the baby was a boy,

```
I felt a sense of loss, even grief, over
my lost daughter. I felt like she's been
replaced by a stranger even though log-
ically I knew that I was carrying the
same baby the whole time, I suddenly felt
really disconnected from my pregnancy.
```

It's not as if gender disappointment, which is really sex disappointment, is a new disappointment invented by ultrasound. Henry VIII had such a bad case of sex disappointment he put off his first wife and created the Church of England because she disappointed him with only a girl baby. His second wife lost her head after giving him only a girl baby and a miscarried boy. Japanese peasant families in the eighteenth century practiced infanticide since too many girls or sometimes too many boys could create disappointing living conditions. Most of the infants killed were girls, although boy babies would be killed, too, if the family already had too many boys or if the last baby to die naturally was a girl, since it was thought bad fortune could come from the deaths of two infants of the same sex one after the other in the same family. The Indian government has passed laws prohibiting sex identification of fetuses during antenatal imaging, but some say that half a million female fetuses so disappoint their ante-parents, they are aborted each year even with the bans in place. Many, IVF clinics may promote sex-selected embryos as a way of avoiding gender disappointment. For the already gender disappointed or those hoping to avoid gender disappointment there is the website called genderdreaming.com.

Worthy of the Event

✺

There I am in an alcove at Sea Life Munich. There I am almost public, getting almost effective cunnilingus with a view of a tank of octopus mostly trying to hide, beautiful. There I am holding hands with Daisuke in Osaka while we watch big-belly seahorses move through pearly water vertical and, since seahorses sort of disprove some of the human cant about fixed sex and gender roles and distinctions (the males bear the children) I finally come out to Daisuke, which means we never hold hands again, but go straight to groaning sexual encounters in love hotels in Takatsuki, near Shinsaibashi, along the main road at Katsura, very disappointing (*not* the sex), and I do not blame the aquarium itself for short-circuiting the romantic part with Daisuke. That early onset of groaning is not his fault, for there is always something glamorous and melting and libidinous, irresistible about those sea creatures in theatrical waters.

Any aquarium seems anything but disappointing, always beautiful to me for years and years until I buy a pen from a serious little boy on the black sand beach at Lovina on the north coast of Bali. Upon the success of his pen-selling skills, the serious little boy carts me off to meet his father, I-Wayan, who is a fisherman with a small, red, white, yellow, and blue jukung outrigger canoe. I-Wayan offers Harry and me a snorkeling trip including breakfast and equipment, and I promise him we have snorkeled before. I do not add that my previous snorkeling was in the tranquil, domestic waters of Hanauma Bay and inside the reef at Kaimana Beach, I don't know about Harry. "Come back to here at four tomorrow morning," the serious little boy says.

At four tomorrow morning, night lies yet thick upon the sea, there is no breeze. We putter off into the dark on a blue cloud of two-stroke, but after an hour heading north, the sky turns as pale as water and a breeze comes up riffling and I-Wayan raises the sail and kills the engine. His serious little boy lights a Sterno and fries tiny bananas in coconut oil, four eggs, and puts one fried banana and one fried egg on top of each of four neat domes of pre-cooked rice on white melamine plates already marked by hot spots of sambal ulek. We eat. I-Wayan eats with one hand on the tiller and the jukung sails on, lateens stiff and straining, and the sea runs thick, it runs slow, it shines, and a pod of dolphin, their curving backs like rainbows in the morning light, trundle along with us making eye contact until I-Wayan lowers the sail and drops the anchor, which is a great lump of coral tied to the end of a rope, and it is quiet, quiet, quiet; to the north, only the Bali Sea, to the south, not much of Bali itself, mostly the cone of Gunung Merbuk, no more than a watermark on the far sky.

"Dive here," I-Wayan says, and when we say, "Really?" he nods and grins, and over the side I go into the open sea, and under, and oh, look, great crania of brain coral dappled by sunlight, throngs of reef fish watching me sideways, surge zones thick with bubbles where swim tuna as mirrored as chromed doorhandles on cars, a sea turtle, a small school of hammerhead sharks indolent in the warm water, and beneath, where the light fights to shine, deep beneath, deep

beyond deep deeply seductive or terrifying or both, a sirenic deep, the ocean drops into the planet and is as calling as a mountain cliff in the Sangre de Cristo is calling jump, jump, come to me. Back on the boat, Harry has jeweled eyelashes and says, "It's an aquarium," but I know without knowing that where I have just been and how that place where I have just been lives, its being, is nothing like an aquarium as I know aquarium, and I am disappointed in myself, not about getting a girl blow job where a tank of cephalopods may see me, but disappointed, crushed really, to see what I had not seen, disappointed to have found any kind of pleasure and beauty in artificial oceans and the enslavement of fish and
boom
and I spend months in the library in Mānoa Valley not reading about Japanese colonialism reading but reading whatever I find on the effects of life in tanks: aquaria are carceral and unnatural in their nature; the marine beings in them are half laboratory specimens, half clowns or strippers, entertainers, they cannot live naturally and are forced to change their ways. Marine animals that hunt, forage, and mate at night are forced into the light; all aquarium creatures must do the day shift. They hurt when you take them out of the water. They hurt when you put a hook in their mouths or gills, chop their heads off, stick needles in them to draw blood, perform vivisections on them. Jellyfish, mollusks, sea snails, anemones, crabs, shrimp, sea slugs, eels, sea horses, even corals may feel pain, hate being looked at, dream of escape. Whale sharks and sea horses and everything in aquaria between whale sharks and sea

horses, the great to the minute, live in fear, traumatized and subjected. It's all hurt in the aquarium, it's all slave labor for the fish. It's all power and specularity for the scientists, the owners of the aquaria, and for you and me each time we go to gawk at wondrous, go to wonder and maybe cop a feel in the shadows, a little kiss or whatever.

I read that the big aquarium in Okinawa captured an adult great white shark and put it on display. Then I read the shark died after four days, dead after four days swimming in circles and butting its great head agonizingly against the glass because you can't put great white sharks into captivity. They always die of disappointment as well as other things like incarceration and not eating and not hunting and not being able to breathe. I wrote a letter to the big aquarium in Okinawa asking them to prohibit such things, and Fairy said, "What are you writing," and when I told her, she said, "You should be prohibited. Kiss me,"

At that point with Fairy, I might've been safer kissing a scorpion fish, but wet mwah anyway.

※

"You can tell me one hundred, I dunno, ten thousand stories but you can't pull the wool over the eyes of Births, Deaths and Marriages," the clerk behind the glass said when I applied for an identity document showing my new legal name. "You reckon you're a bit smart, doncha, using 'a' for Vivian instead of 'e' and I don't care if 'a' *is* the British spelling for men who are Vivians, I mean, men Vivians, get out, look at yourself, it's obvious you're one of those transsexuals and the government of this state is not going to give you any document to help you hoodwink people into thinking you're a woman or whatever the heck it is you're trying to be, and it's no good telling me any different. It's no good, neither, telling me I'm breaking the law. We do have a policy," and then he said he was sorry, and sometimes people were, but not him.

I tried the next day. No.

I tried another day with a different clerk. No.

"It seems unjust to me, and illegal," I said, polite.

No, but a less kind no than the previous no and absent the apology.

"Births, Deaths and Marriages is not going to help you further your delusion."

I spent each day there in the waiting room at the Federation Gothic building built of golden Sydney sandstone. I applied. The clerk said no. I asked why. The clerk gave the reason. I objected. The clerk insisted. I took out my copy of *The Iliad* and sat for two hours then repeated the application refusal cycle again and again until closing time and the next day the next day the next day the next day. "You are acting illegally," I would say, "I have not asked you to change my sex on my papers and as you admit yourselves, my new name is the male version with an 'a', capital V-i-v-i-a-n, I demand to speak with the registrar-general, how am I expected to live."

On the Tuesday of the second week, two cops arrived hairy or determined to be hairy in navy blue, a big one and a reedy one. At least one smelled of Old Spice. They planted themselves in front of me. They asked me to leave. No. They warned me of consequences, but I was then and am now undaunted by consequences of almost any kind so: no. The reedy one pulled me gently into the base notes of benzoin and cedar, almost an embrace, it was, with his pink face in my breasts because he was short, and he spun me around and frog-marched me out and deposited me into Queen's Square. "I'm not a queen," I said, "put me out on Prince Albert Road at least."

"Har-har. Then what are yer," the big cop said from some backup position. "Whatever it is, stop it."

After that, day eight, day nine, the same: ask for the paper of identity, dispute the refusal, sit, two cops, until on the morning of day ten, Friday, I got tired of it, I got disappointed at the repetitious character of political activism and I put on my crocheted purple bikini and a lot of waterproof tape, very much later, and I went to Wattamolla Beach with Mitchell and I took a tiny pane of acid and jumped from the cliff into the mysterious water over and over again, laughing in the glittering sun.

※

Lana Luxemburg fled Bundaberg where it is subtropical, where they give bananas away, where they distill rum, and where Lana Luxemburg's father was a labor organizer for sugar industry workers and, according to Lana Luxemburg, a fucking Stalinist, and we were both still kids, really; me, seventeen although I always said eighteen unless to the cops who preferred to avoid at all costs entanglement in the business of charging a minor with one, two, three, or all of soliciting money for sexual acts, public indecency, offensive behavior, consorting with known criminals, loitering, vagrancy, failing to heed police instructions. Lana Luxemburg was about eighteen and a half, and we ended up sharing a room at the back of a house next to a shelter for unhoused men. I said, "Isn't Luxembourg a duchy between some big countries in Europe?"

Lana Luxemburg said, "Don't try to be a clever, it doesn't suit you. It's not my legal name but, if you must know, I am not the Luxembourg with an o, I am Luxemburg without the o as in *the* Rosa Luxemburg Luxemburg."

Then Lana Luxemburg told me the story of how *the* Rosa Luxemburg Luxemburg had been at the vanguard of an outright socialist revolution begun in Germany in 1917 by sailors sick of World War I and finished in 1919 by the Prussian aristocracy and industrialists fully weaponized by military units known as Freikorps. She told me how *the* Rosa Luxemburg Luxemburg had been bashed in the head and shot by two officers of a Freikorps unit in Berlin, her body dumped in a canal. "But her revolutionary thought lives on in me," Lana Luxemburg said, and then she looked at herself in the mirror, full face, left profile, right profile, and said, "I must be adopted. Nobody in Bundaberg has a nose like this, how disappointing this nose is."

And it must be said, we all said it, Lana Luxemburg did have a disappointing nose. She had a more than disappointing nose. Lana Luxemburg had a terrible nose. Her nose was so bad, she did dozens of tricks night and day, if she could, and then put the money in a special Commonwealth Bank of Australia savings account, Lana Luxemburg called My Beauty Account. As far as I was concerned, even with that disappointing actually terrible nose, Lana Luxemburg was the most attractive girl-like-I-am-girl girl I had yet met. It might have been her dedication to *doing* Rosa Luxemburg's spontaneity and creativity in revolutionary action that I liked so much, I mean, I see now that Lana Luxemburg's spontaneously creative revolutionary actions mostly amounted to screaming "Your end is fucking coming!" *etcetera* at astonished men in bespoke suits and shocked women in expensive dresses, hats, and gloves outside David Jones department store on Elizabeth Street or waiting for a cab at the main entrance of the Chevron Hotel, and after screaming, running off shrieking, pointless really, but the looks of consternation on the faces of those people we called the Squares made me love Lana Luxemburg more than I thought I could love Lana Luxemburg.

The aircraft carrier, *USS America*, hit Sydney from South Vietnam. Lana Luxemburg put on a full face and new false eyelashes and my chrome-yellow sundress with the spaghetti straps, her hair glossy, black, up, and she went out into the night to make some **real** money. She was visualizing rhinoplasty, another four hundred to go, tonight is nose job money night. "See you later tonight," Lana Luxemburg said, but she didn't come home later that night. I didn't find her fastidious over eggs and rösti at Una's in the morning. I didn't find Lana Luxemburg turning tricks on Riley or

Boomerang streets the next night, either. Where was Lana Luxemburg? "Don't ask me," Big Denise said, "There's a smorgasbord of American servicemen with a ton of money in town and they've been at sea or in the jungles so long, they're not fussy about a nose. What do you think? Maybe she got a three-day deal and she's flown up to Surfer's Paradise with some gorgeous chief petty officer, you know, like Annette did that time."

It turned out Lana Luxemburg was not enjoying the breakers and making three-hundred a day up at Surfer's Paradise. Lana was floating in the water. She was bobbing limp and sodden. She was bumping gently dead against the seawall around Bennelong Point where the new Sydney Opera House was in the middle of hoisting its concrete sails and soon *Aida* or *Werther* and *Swan Lake*, and I heard from the vice squad detective we all called Mr. Plod, for a good reason, that Lana Luxemburg's nose appeared to have been punched right into her face, and I heard that Lana Luxemburg's Stalinist labor organizer father refused to acknowledge Lana Luxemburg as his child and left her to be buried in the Australian version of a potters' field. He was unworthy of the event. Lana Luxemburg would want you to know that.

※

The Rosa Luxemburg Luxemburg is in prison again, this time for two and a half years. She is in German prisons in Posen and Breslau for the crime of writing illegal antiwar pamphlets signed "Spartakus". She has reasons to be disappointed, although not in her incarceration, which, as always, Rosa Luxemburg uses to write increasingly acute and visionary polemics and to clear her thinking. Even locked up, Rosa Luxemburg will not allow disappointment to board the vessel of her revolution, not only because to be disappointed is to be defeated, but because revolutionaries, particularly socialist revolutionaries, do not allow themselves any expectation of personal satisfaction accrued from their revolutionary activities. The only expectation Rosa Luxemburg allows Rosa Luxemburg is solidarity with comrades, from which grows commitment to political activism and the ability to make personal sacrifices for the future. She has no room in all this for disappointment.

In a letter almost as loving as it is scathing, composed in a cell at Wronke Prison outside Posen (Poznan), Rosa Luxemburg excoriates her close friend and political comrade, Mathilde Wurm: My dear Tilde, I am answering your Christmas letter immediately, while I still feel the wrath it caused me. Your letter made me terribly, wildly angry, because, for all its brevity, every line of it shows that you have again totally succumbed to the environment in which you move. This tearfully complaining tone, this self-pity and wailing over the 'disappointments' you have suffered — you say you have been disappointed in others, but why not look into the mirror, where you might discover the whole misery of mankind accurately portrayed. **And:** It is fortunate that the history of humanity was not made by people like you, or there would have been no Reformation and we would probably still be living under the Ancien Regime. But so far as I am concerned, while I have never been soft, I have recently become as hard as polished steel and from now on I will not make the slightest concession, either politically or in personal relations.

Yet, after more indignant railing against disappointment and its companions, Rosa Luxemburg turns all warm, almost gooey she goes, and she offers Mathilde Wurm a method for managing disappointment. She tries to teach Mathilde Wurm a way of being worthy of the event: To be a Mensch, that is the main thing. And that means to remain steadfast, clear, serene; yes, serene despite everything. To whimper is the business of weaklings. To be a Mensch means gladly to throw one's whole life, when need be, onto the 'great scale of destiny.' And it means, as well, to find pleasure in each clear day and each beautiful cloud.

Had she lived to see the Stalinist version of the Union of Soviet Socialist Republics, Rosa Luxemburg might have been disappointed in revolution altogether. She might have needed to do something to elevate that philosophy of the mensch to account for how disappointing revolutions become. Dear old Theda Skocpol showed us long ago that the great modern revolutions in France, the United States, Russia, and China eventually fell back into new forms of authority and new elites encrusted with the right to power, which disappointed the revolutionaries themselves and disappointed large numbers of the citizenry, who could not be blamed for thinking that the future promised by the revolution now looked rather like the past. But politics is a game of disappointment, how to be I-am-not-disappointed-it-is-the-will-of-the-people and how to be worthy of the disappointment when it comes inevitable, how not be crushed, and how to rise again and just keep trying to win, that is politics, or life itself.

※

Girls like me are not expected to be disappointed by our vaginas even for a second and, if girls like me *are* disappointed by our vaginas once we've got our vaginas (and vulvas, okay), we are not supposed to talk about the disappointment because this is a success story. Girls like me *are* permitted, even required, it seems, to feel existential and social and financial disappointment because the marks upon the subjectivity of girls like me are deep, there is no way around *that*, deep enough often enough to impoverish us, get us fired, lifetimes of stress and then that myocardial infarction in front of the bathroom mirror while mascara, how disappointing, except that girls like me are often good at disappointment. Girls like me learn not *not* to be disappointed; we learn how to be worthy of it. We learn to dilute disappointment and wash it down the drain, how to scrape disappointment off without abrasion several times a day or how to walk past disappointment looking fabulous or how to turn disappointment into a bit worthy of *us*.

We are: Like all men in Babylon I have been a proconsul; like all, a slave; I have also known omnipotence, opprobrium, jail. Look: the index finger of my right hand is missing. Look again: through this rent in my cape you can see a ruddy tattoo on my belly. It is the second symbol, Beth. This letter, on nights of full moon, gives me power over men whose mark is Ghimel; but it also subordinates me to those marked Aleph, who on moonless nights owe obedience to those marked Ghimel. In a cellar at dawn, I have severed the jugular vein of sacred bulls against a black rock. During one lunar year, I have been declared invisible: I shrieked and was not heard, I stole my bread and was not decapitated. I have known what the Greeks did not: uncertainty. In a bronze chamber, faced with the silent handkerchief of a strangler, hope has been faithful to me; in the river of delights, panic has not failed me. Heraclitus of Pontica admiringly relates that Pythagoras recalled having been Pyrrho, and before that Euphorbus, and before that some other mortal. In order to recall analogous vicissitudes, I do not need to have recourse to death, nor even to imposture.

Look at me: I am riven and formed. I am lost and I am found within my own Babylon and from my own relationships to the power I do have and to the power I do not have; power today, gone powerless tomorrow, I am. I am master and servant and everything in between. Lord, lady, maiden, equerry, squire, yeoman, and serf. I am abuser and victim of abuse. See me ugly, plain, sort of okay, a seven, very attractive, beautiful, drop-dead gorgeous. I am made and I exist in an ambivalent association of ideas about my right to speak and the need to shut the fuck up, my right to own *and* how much has been taken from me, what I want and what I am not ever allowed to have, hold me, don't touch me, get out, come, I know and I do not know, and always always always always **watch your back**. I do not need to have recourse to death, and when my own black star shows up for me, I will be worthy of it.

And even now, after a lot, even now, so far along in all the restless becoming that seems to be the hallmark of human being, even now, there are triumphs, there are disappointments to be had and to remember and, oh, I feel them, but I am not disappointed. I am not disappointed with how long it took me to understand the effects of all those insults and hits and objectifications and jokes and dismissals and stereotypes. It is not disappointing to fear myself, it is logical. I was a disappointment in every marriage and in every love affair between every marriage and some not between at all, but I am not disappointed by any of that. I've taken and given a lot of disappointing fucks; who has not. I know what I have done. Those flighty ways with my academic career disappointed at least two mentors who imagined me and my scholarly bottom comfortably endowed in a chair and an office with a view of Indianapolis or some patch of shriveled and raucous Australian bush or even those vegetating suburbs between Kyoto and Osaka. Many people would be disappointed to reach this age and still not own their home, and I have been, but I am not now. I have often craved more light than ever fell on me, and that mostly unsatisfied craving might have led to disappointment except that every time they ask me to speak up about anything on radio or television, make a video for some literary prize I will not win, give a speech at some university, even present research at a conference, terror gets me hard, it is dry, **water!** and there I am in the light I wanted, tongue-tied or too sharp or overly facetious, and too much lipstick, so I am not disappointed about that, I am *private*. I am marked, mark me. There have been disappointments. I am not disappointed. All has been and is now as it could be or it is what I made of could-be after I gave up on Pastor Bullock, fire and brimstone, resurrection, and God the Fucking Father at the Coleman Street Seventh-Day Adventist Church.

✳

Baruch Spinoza advises understanding disappointment itself, although he never gives a method or even explains what disappointment *itself* might be that is different from disappointment *myself*. Gottfried Leibniz wants us to give yours mine theirs that and this disappointment up to a higher power, which, in his view, is a version of God not Baruch Spinoza's God the Substance but God the Super-Father in which Gottfried Leibniz is able to be
```
perfectly content when I am not successful,
being convinced that... it is for the
best, as currently God does not will it.
I do my part so long as there is hope, and
I am content with His part when there is
hope no longer.
```
Then there is the early Confucian technique for disappointment: there is li or etiquette. Proper etiquette, properly done, refines us, sharpens one and all as the whetstone refines and sharpens a knife. The early Confucian etiquette for disappointment is to practice civility, good manners, proper conduct, do the rituals, for, just as feelings shape outer behavior and social affects, outer behavior shapes inner emotions and affects. When disappointment comes and we feel it badly and we lack good manners for it, disappointment blunts, diminishes, and distorts positive feelings about colleagues, about that rejecting publisher, that university search committee, that queer community, that panel of judges for the Man Booker Prize, that "no, I'm not in love with you", that "go away", that awful world. Upon such disappointments, our sociality becomes indisposed, those early Confucians might say. The proper response then is to

restore our sociality to good health. This is not accomplished by wild parties, raving, a cocaine fest with friends at a club, a weekend in a luxury suite at the Shangri-la, drunk on Kuta Beach, leaving what happened in Vegas in Vegas, not a shopping spree, not even a seven-day silent retreat at Spirit Rock, what fun, but no. Restore the positive tenor of your feelings, those early Confucians say, by keeping your disappointed mouth shut as much as possible. Practice civility instead, they say, allow li to make society happy and happy society will make *you* happy. Be polite. Mind your language. Express courtesy to, and pleasure in, your acquaintances, friends, and family rather than disappointment. Attend to happy birthday, congratulations, weddings, parties, funerals, graduation ceremonies. Be respectful to all rituals and routines including the rituals and routines of animals. Weed and water the garden. Volunteer. Attend. Look after the planet. Saying thank you is more important than talking about gratitude. Do to be. Practice reliable grace. "That is all very well, civil and graceful," says Norma Mapagu, "but wishy-washy. Give me an example."

Example: "Nothing happens," the 16th Gyalwang Karmapa says in English just before he dies. It sounds a hopeless sort of thing to say on a death bed, but the 16th Gyalwang Karmapa's visitors, who are all monks from his inner circle, smile and laugh, and grief beams on their faces like ten thousand suns in a noonday sky as their beloved leader slips away. They disappoint no one. They no longer know how to be disappointed. The enjoy themselves in the event. They enjoy the event. They are worthy of it.

II: mouse eats communion wafer

I am not a philosopher no matter how philosophical I may become after one too many, upon disaster, looking back. For example, I know the meaning of ontology, but I don't understand the difference between being and becoming. Pushed on it, I might say being is an abstraction about things, identities, conditions, and existences that cannot and do not change: the color red, for instance, to which, in the abstract, nothing happens.

Becoming, I might say, is where life occurs: red fades to pink. Becoming is all happening. Being is you locked in as you. Becoming is you unlocked. Becoming `is the power of specifically growing out of one's self, of making the past and the strange one body with the near and present,` I might say, not really understanding what is being, what is becoming, parroting something I've read. Yet, without understanding, I know what being is and is not, what becoming is and is not. I *feel* it. I live it. Years after I stop being important to Harry and he to me, Harry says, "There is something incessant about you. All the names and identities and careers and countries and marriages or similar and appearances and attitudes and enthusiasms or not. I could never catch you."

I could say but I do not say, "That is pretty much the point."

※

On Facebook and Insta and TikTok some people carefully or without care, willy-nilly or deliberately, inadvertently or they've got a plan, and any combination of intent and its opposites, document themselves becoming who they really are or who they want to be or what they must be or how they want and don't want to be. I've watched people sicken and die on socials, go geriatric, become mothers, thin, fat, adults, stars, citizens of countries other than their birthplaces, become memories and traces. With a bit of industrious scrolling on Facebook, you can track the look of McKenzie Wark becoming woman just as, with more industrious scrolling back back back, you can watch the McKenzie Wark brand shuck off a lot of its Australian and become American in a not-quite-Manhattan kind of way American. Like all of us, McKenzie Wark is both an unchanging abstraction and a constant unlocking of herself to become something and somehow else.

McKenzie Wark's becoming woman is not hard to understand. You can see it happening on her platforms. She is floral. She burgeons like an early summer garden, shooting, sprouting, busting out of herself, budding, blossoming, effulgent, verging on winsome, and increasingly pretty. In those pictures, McKenzie Wark's breasts and ass/arse have not yet quite popped. They may never pop. She may always have to cock a leg to get a hip in a selfie, and this stubborn angularity may disappoint her, I don't know, but if leanness where she doesn't want it casts her down, McKenzie Wark should see how her skin illuminates itself from within. She should see how her lips have gone red and almost pouty. She should see how a slim layer of estrogen fat *implies* undulation at all her angles. She should see how all those pills and all those intramuscular hypodermic applications shine on her like extra-virgin spritzed on green beans and toasted almonds, glisten her like that final mist of liquefied duck fat turns a well-plated entrée to satin at Spruce on Sacramento Street, if you can afford it, so inviting, although McKenzie Wark is not becoming a duck, and if you've read *Reverse Cowgirl*, you'll know she's no virgin, front or back, top or bottom, and other places I may not know about, although my not knowing all the body places up for some form of copulation is unlikely. I am experienced, and I've become like McKenzie Wark becomes, except the social platform part: announced and stuffed with estrogen and depilated, zapped hairless until the thick sheen of dupioni silk, transformed orgasms, weeping nipples, breasts hurting so bad they cannot be slept on, center of gravity moving south, skin turning inside out, the curve of the eye changing. "Your vision has improved," the optometrist says, not ironically, although I could never see what lay ahead. It was mostly unplanned.

Worthy of the Event

Does McKenzie Wark see where she is going? Is there a map for her becoming or does she *feel* her way along? When will she be finished? Étienne Souriau might enquire. Does McKenzie Wark have some stop up ahead there at which she gets off becoming herself and enters a state of being, or is her becoming, and all becoming, the true condition of life? Does leaving ourselves for other ourselves define the human condition? Does becoming go on and on and on and on unstopping, never reaching being? Is there any end to it?

If life occurs in the becoming and not in the being of us, there might be no being beyond becoming, nothing beyond multiplicity; no essences beyond appearance. And if becoming is the basic condition of human life, why do some people, even *good* people get angry, anxious, confused, critical, suspicious, hurt, scornful and punishing about some kinds of becoming yet admiring and enthusiastic about other kinds of becoming? Who can honestly say they don't enjoy a becoming rich famous successful loved gorgeous cancer-free and educated happy US Australia Canada UK Germany Netherlands France NZ citizen story? But when the story is becoming a woman man neither in defiance of what is said on your birth document, enjoy is harder to find. You can't change biology, those anxious angry hating people say. What about chromosomes. No matter how many fucking pills you fucking take and no matter how much surgery you have you can't become a woman. Get real. But if Friedrich Nietzsche, Martin Heidegger, and Gilles Deleuze (to name just a few) are right about becoming being the real term of human life rather than a subordinate clause of being, then all that discomfort and horror and loathing about people becoming what you think they are not supposed to be is just a fight against life itself.

I do not say that me becoming a woman or McKenzie Wark becoming a woman or *you* becoming a woman when it says something different on your papers is a solution to anything except yourself, but some becomings *do* have policy implications. The greatest power of the Polynesian demigod, Māui, is to become inhuman in order to manage human problems. Māui becomes bird, worm, or insect mostly. Sometimes people throw things at Māui when he is become bird. Some don't quite trust him. They feel his becoming bird or worm or insect might be a nasty trick, and Māui does sometimes seem to be mocking them, but his becoming bird becoming insect becoming worm protects and grows the aina, the reciprocal political, social, and cultural relationship between Māui's people and the land upon which the success of everything relies. Māui's becomings solve and make things, create Aotearoa New Zealand, Tonga, fire, dogs, and death (which is a benefit in the disguise of tragedy). Whether Māui becomes *like* a bird, *like* an insect, and *like* a worm or becomes *a* bird, *an* insect, or *a* worm seems unimportant in the stories. Gods and demigods don't often bother with the questions of whether real is like or real is real, whether actual is fiction or fiction is actual, and impossibility might not be and should not be in any god's vocabulary.

Worthy of the Event

✸

At Pastor Bullock's church on Coleman Street, the coming apocalypse was very real, but the communion wine was grape juice, the communion wafer was a saltine cracker without the salt. Pastor Bullock talked a lot about the body and blood of Jesus Christ: `And when he had given thanks, he brake it, and said, Take, eat: this is my body, which is broken for you: this do in remembrance of me. After the same manner also he took the cup, when he had supped, saying, this cup is the new testament in my blood: this do ye, as oft as ye drink it, in remembrance of me.` But Pastor Bullock also made it clear to his flock (us) that the squares of dreary saltine wannabe and the stale thimbles of dark grape juice were symbolic, they were *representations* of the body and blood of Our Savior, not the Son of God's actual body and blood themselves. "We are better than that," Pastor Bullock said.

Not better than that: those Catholic girls from Mount Erin Boarding School for Girls and their Catholic families out on sheep and wheat near Mangoplah and Holbrook. Not better than that: those kids at Saint Maria Goretti and Bishop Henschke Boys with family names like Toohey and di Marco who were inclined to think that when they got to do Holy Communion they would be really biting into the actual body of Christ, really slurping up his real blood. Even as the town dropped reluctantly into the age of disbelief and agonized over getting a discotheque on Leichhardt Street, sending twenty-year-old men to fight an American war in Vietnam, The Pill, and men on the moon, there were those who clung to the medieval belief that whenever heathens, or even Protestants (!) bit into the Eucharist wafer with pagan or Reformation sentiments in their hearts, the wafer would bleed the actual blood of Jesus Christ. Spurt. The thirteenth-century efforts of Thomas Aquinas, Bonaventure, and Albertus Magnus to convince the faithful that the Son of God did not *become* a flour-and-water wafer, that the flour-and-water wafer did not become the living, breathing, shitting, sweating, horny human body within which the Son of God had briefly conducted his life on earth, did not reach so many in that town where I grew up.

To be honest, the difference between symbolic Jesus blood, symbolic Jesus body and real Jesus blood and body did not reach many in Europe in the 1200s, either. The difference between sacramentum and sensorium was lost on most then. Medieval communicants felt the flesh between their teeth, the little gush of warm, red blood upon their tongues IRL. After all, why not flour and water to actual blood and flesh? Consider water into wine at Cana, death into life for Lazarus, loaves of bread and silvery fish dividing and dividing and dividing until the five thousand are fed and belching upon the shore of Galilee. Jesus-become-actual-Jesus-in-a-wafer seemed acceptable, even desirable to communicants, and the Church thought so too, really, and began mounting Jesus-Christ-become-wafer in monstrances, extravagant crystal display cases framed by

Worthy of the Event

precious metals and thickly studded with gems. In the museum at the Igreja de São Francisco do Porto, there is one such monstrance: thick gold, gems encrusted, and a crystal case for Christ-become-wafer, wafer-become-Christ. In a better world, the living become-woman body of McKenzie Wark would be set in that crystal case, draped in gold and huge, pigeon's-egg rubies and emerald-cut diamonds and carried high above crowds blessed beyond their wildest dreams by the sight of what is possible.

According to G.W.F. Hegel, if a mouse eats Jesus-Christ-become-wafer or wafer-become-Jesus-Christ, then God exists in the mouse, exists even in the shit of the mouse. In contrast to McKenzie Wark's embodied becoming, the form of the mouse goes on unchanged by its becoming but the inner being of the pilfering mouse becomes transformed, divine. Baruch Spinoza might have thought Hegel's mouse, inside and out, and everything else in the universe, inside and out, were all God modes, inside and out, since God is a universal substance with a zillion ways of being, infinite articulations, uncountable and unknowable, one of which might be Hegel's mouse-become-God – well, anyway, Hegel's proposition that mouse-eating-consecrated-wafer becomes God got Hegel into hot water with the Prussian state. After all, just who in Berlin then was going to accept a rodent as God and offer it their whining, pleading supplications on bended knee and hymns and reverence instead of out with the Kaput Rat & Mouse Bait or whatever Prussians used on sacrilegious mice in the early 1800s. Arsenic, I suppose, and you are a mouse, not God, you are a man, not a woman, you cannot become what you are not: pass the poison.

✴

    Nothing about becoming seems to have worried Gertrude Stein. It was being she did not care for: `I am thinking of attacking being not as an earthy kind of substance but as a pulpy not dust not dirt but a more mixed up substance, it can be slimy, gelatinous, gluey, white opaquy kind of thing and it can be white and vibrant, and clear and heated and this is all not very clear to me`, Gertrude Stein writes in *The Making of Americans*, which is her most becoming work, the work in which she shows herself becoming Gertrude Stein the author we know now.

✴

    In one or two pictures, McKenzie Wark wears a black mini skirt printed with white katakana. I DM her: ru turning Japanese? Lol.
    She is not. McKenzie Wark has enough on her becoming plate right now.
    She DMs: `It's just a weeb aesthetic.`
    Weeb: `You know the type — foreigners who are so deep down the rabbit hole that they want to` *become* `Japanese. They can be seen using Japanese words incorrectly, dressing up like anime characters, and`

```
worshipping Japan without knowing anything
about  it  outside  what  they've  seen  in
anime.
```
That woman from The Hague was anything but weeb. She was intent on not becoming Japanese. She had been living in Kyoto for twenty-three years, and she said over Yebisu and pizza with octopus arms, or are they feet, "I am *completely* illiterate in the Japanese language. That is my choice."

With a whip of blonde plait and a delft-blue glare, she dared me to expostulate. She said, "I don't care what people think. I am proud not to understand nor speak a single word of Japanese," although I once heard her say a perfect two words, arigatō gozaimasu, to an usher who had given her a better seat at that performance space for the avant-garde of Kyoto and foreigners like me and this Dutch woman who thought living in Kyoto made us avant-garde too.

The woman from The Hague said, "This way Japan is all just good or bad design and sound effects to me, it is all art, and I can go about my business undistracted. I just want the aesthetic."

I said, "It might be okay to know how to say in Japanese, 'Do you have a condom?'"

"Language is the mainspring of identity," she said. "Why even start? It would be easier for me to become a man than to become Japanese, you know that. It is hard for even Japanese to become Japanese."

•

Becoming a man is hard and unstopping, even for legally-male-from-day-one men. Becoming a man if you were identified as female on day one is harder, anywhere. It is a journey in time and body through feeling, thinking, relationships, looks, and culture. And no matter how far you go, some people and organizations won't accept it. If you want to make your becoming man official in The Netherlands, official being a prerequisite of believable, you need a medical certificate prepared by a deskundige transgenders, a transgender expert, but you are no longer required to have taken testosterone, had your tits removed, had your ovaries, womb, and vagina removed, had a cock put on. You submit the transgender-expert medical certificate to the town where you were born, which changes your birth certificate, and you use the new birth certificate to change your record in the National Personal Records Database upon which all other government records rely. Done.

Big Denise went to get her birth certificate changed but Records Clerk said, "What are you thinking? We can't accept some certificate from Thailand or any of those places where anything can be faked up by anybody with a Xerox machine, and if you can't certify vagina, you can't be a woman here, that's for sure."

The government required Big Denise to submit to vaginal inspection by two Australian doctors and a duly authorized officer of the state sheriff's office. One of the two doctors said he was so very sorry about it, although he turned out not sorry enough to keep his hand off and his forefinger out. The other doctor refused to examine and stood at a distance training his eyes on the sphygmomanometer to the left of Big Denises's head, which, at that time, was crowned by a deluxe tumble of copper curls. The duly authorized sheriff showed up wearing a uniform and a gun. He kept his right hand on his gun when he peered at Big Denise's neovagina. **Bang**. He also put his lips into an O and put his wide and marbled eyes on Big Denise's pussy so hard it was as though he were looking at the eighth wonder of the world.

Big Denise took the medical certificate to the right window, where Records Clerk said, "It'll be ready for you in ten business days. Or less."

Big Denise felt non-sequiturial so she said to the Records Clerk, "I am a woman."

Records Clerk checked the calendar and said, "Not until November 8, you're not."

After the ten business days, Big Denise folded the new birth certificate with F on it in the right place into a large origami crane. "I will become a German poet now," she said. "That will be easier than this."

It was not.

I consulted Psychiatrist Haik about a bad case of yearning. Psychiatrist Haik said, "Well, now you've become a woman, sort of, do you really need to attempt another impossibility?"

I said, "I want to go to university and study history, get a Ph.D. and become a university professor or something like that."

Psychiatrist Haik said, "You will be very unhappy if your life continues as a sequence of vainglorious efforts to become something other than what you are. Let's meet weekly for the next six months and we can work on ways for you to be happy and content with you being you."

Koizumi Yakumo was still Lafcadio Hearn when he came to Japan in 1890, but he started becoming Koizumi Yakumo almost as soon as he set foot on the streets of Setagaya, and becoming Koizumi Yakumo only quickened after he moved to the northwest coast town of Matsue and married Koizumi Setsuko and changed his name to Koizumi Yakumo. He really yearned to become Japanese: `I feel indescribably towards Japan. Of course, Nature here is not the Nature of the tropics, which is so splendid and savage and omnipotently beautiful that I feel at this very moment of writing the same pain in my heart I felt when leaving Martinique. This is a domesticated Nature, which loves man, and makes itself beautiful for him in a quiet grey-and-blue way like the Japanese women, and the trees seem to know what people say about them, — seem to have little human souls. What I love in Japan is the Japanese, — the poor simple humanity of the country. It is divine. There is nothing in this world approaching the naïve natural charm of them. No book ever written has reflected it. And I love their gods, their customs, their dress, their bird-like quavering songs, their houses, their superstitions, their faults. And I believe that their art is as far in advance of our art as old Greek art was superior to`

> that of the earliest European art — gropings —
> I think there is more art in a print
> by Hokusai or those who came after him
> than in a $10,000 painting — no, a $100,000
> painting. *We* are the barbarians! I do not
> merely *think* these things: I am as sure of
> them as of death. I only wish I could be
> reincarnated in some little Japanese baby,
> so that I could see and feel the world as
> beautifully as a Japanese brain does.

Basil Hall Chamberlain, who was to become one of the grand old men of the Western academic study of Japan, was disgusted. "You don't have to go that far with these women," he said and sprinkled his starched shirt front with a little 4711 because the day was torrid in Tokyo.

The other expatriates said Koizumi Yakumo had gone native, how disgusting, deplorable, well what would you expect, after all, they say, wasn't he was married to a black woman in Louisiana or somewhere awful. They refused to refer to him as anything other than Lafcadio Hearn. Even now, Westerners call Koizumi Yakumo Lafcadio Hearn and regard his becoming Japanese as the kind of impossible dream within which old men sometimes lose themselves, especially in Asia. In Japan now, nobody thinks Koizumi Yakumo was Japanese Japanese, but his becoming Japanese is respected, his books are held in great esteem, and he is almost always called Koizumi Yakumo.

·

K had shoulders worth clutching. K was raised in the city of Kōchi but educated in Lexington, Kentucky where he thought of himself as becoming American, but after fifteen years and three diplomatically put refusals of his applications for tenure at a state university in Texas, and after Lolly left him and took the child and went off to Oregon to work as a flight attendant on Air Rajneesh and then fled to somewhere south of Dresden when Rajneeshpuram went very bad; after all that, which was a lot, K with the beautiful shoulders came to Kyoto to live. "I am not becoming Japanese again," he said to me. K told people he was Australian, "I know I look quite, um, Japanese, but I am not, and my Japanese language is impossible," he said, and he refused to speak one word of the language, even in his job. I mean, K wouldn't even say takoyaki. He would say: "These grilled octopus meatballs with a sauce made of Bulldog Worcestershire sauce, soup base, sugar and ketchup and garnished with dried bonito flakes are the best ever."

Don't get me wrong. I am not criticizing the becoming not-Japanese of K, to whose beautiful shoulders I once or twice clung, making noises not in any language.

✺

Martin Heidegger thought we exist in a condition of permanent homesickness, yearning for the home-sweet-home of being, stable and essential. Our yearning is never satisfied, yet we try to find a way home to ourselves again again again again. We: always underway. Underway is us. Just one of Martin Heidegger's underways was becoming a Nazi then becoming not-a-Nazi.

Worthy of the Event

•

Marquis Bey is Professor of Black studies, gender and sexuality studies, and English at Northwestern University. They (or any pronoun) cannot *not* think about Rachel Dolezal, not so much thinking about Rachel Dolezal herself but cannot *not* think about Rachel Dolezal's decades of becoming Black (not African American), rejecting whiteness. Rachel Dolezal was a well-known Black activist. She was a teacher. She was president of the Spokane chapter of the National Association for the Advancement of Colored People (NAACP). Then Rachel Dolezal's white parents told the media Rachel Dolezal was not Black and never had been Black. Marquis Bey *is* Black and African-American and cannot *not* think about the blitzkrieg of denunciation and mockery dropped on Rachel Dolezal when her white mother and father told the media Rachel Dolezal was white-bread born and bred, as white as white can be white except in her head where she *felt* and still *feels*, as far as I know, Black. Even after the storm of outing, Rachel Dolezal never recanted her Blackness, just kept on becoming who she felt she was, although grimly it seems. Marquis Bey cannot *not* think about what Rachel Dolezal forces us to think about the intrinsic underway-ness of sex, gender, and racial categories, and the regulation of those categories, about becoming, about what happens fiercely when one becomes across embodied categories, generations of suffering, and sacred cows. You are not real.

I ask Norma Mapagu: "Would I take something of yours if I identified as Filipino?"

Norma Mapagu says I am too tall to become Filipino. "You'd never pass," she says, and she says she thinks Filipino might hurt me more than it hurts Filipino. "Also, you'd have to learn to say yes when you mean no, learn to say thank you when you want to say fuck off, although, come to think of it, you probably learned some of that becoming a woman."

•

Even now, my sister lets me know in divers ways how much my becoming a woman hurt her, how my sex change robbed her of the respectability for which she yearned. I've had to give my sister up.

•

I once dated a man who didn't tell me he was Black until I had fucked him thirteen and a half times in nice hotel rooms. After he said, "I think you should know I am Black," I thought I had finally found my soulmate and I told him about my sex change, at which tears gathered in his lime-green eyes, and he said I should have told him before we fucked even one time. "I'm not into transes, fake women," he said over crab cake and tempura lobster tail with a view of Prospect Bay lacquered pink and primrose as the sun went down. "You've hurt me. You've robbed me of choice."

We had come in my car, but he was very polite and said he would get a cab back to Bethesda, thank you, and I spent the night alone in an unctuous room at Kent Island Resort where a wedding party got drunk on love.

•

Norma Mapagu says, "Your sister is homesick for something. She is homesick for herself, but she just can't get underway. She can't become herself and blames you for it. She is stuck. She is so stuck she thinks stuck is the way things are. She is so stuck she thinks stuck is who she is. She is so stuck she has to think that anybody becoming anything other than what she thinks they are is breaking the law and hurting her."

※

On the night of December 27th at the house in New Hampshire, Harry's father takes me into the library. "Be seated, dear," he says.

I go onto that sofa covered in a ginkgo-leaf and salamander pattern. Harry's father gives me a thick finger of Dewars in a crystal glass, which I know was his grandmother's crystal glass once in Frankfurt or Manhattan, I'm not clear about the exact where of it, but I do know all sixteen of those antique crystal glasses etched with water lilies might be mine in the future, and a lot more besides, if I stick it out. Don't make mistakes, do not make mistakes is my mantra. Harry's father is in the acid-green wing chair near the fire. Snow sleeves the arms of the hemlocks outside. He says, "You've been trying very hard, haven't you, to become one of the family, and you've been doing very well. We know that. And you know, too, we love you, dear, dearly, we really do, but I have to tell you that *etcetera* is pronounced *et-cet-er-a* not *ek-cet-ra*, I know you don't want to sound common and low class, and you're not, so don't. *Etcetera*."

And we listen to the Brahms Violin Concerto with Itzhak Perlman and the Chicago Symphony, and cottony balls of snow twirl bright in the outside lights, and I, gone craven in my becoming bourgeois, say, "Thank you, Poppa, I am enlightened," and I never say *ekcetra* again, no, never, never, not once.

Also: those antique crystal glasses never come to me, but I do have the cocktail party skills, what is the chocolate spoon and what is the fish fork and what a chocolate spoon is for, and I do have that nineteenth-century Japanese golden silk scroll painting of Bodhidharma who spent nine years facing the wall before becoming enlightened too.

"Your father is an Ishmael," I say. "I am not going to be his Queequeg."

Harry cannot get the reference. I run downstairs, grab a fluorescent-pink highlighter and vandalize the relevant age-proofed page of an American Library edition of *Moby Dick*.

In that this-is-CBS-News voice he has, Harry reads what I've highlighted: `But Queequeg, do you see, was a creature in the transition stage — neither caterpillar nor butterfly. He was just enough civilized to show off his outlandishness in the strangest possible manners. His education was not yet completed. He was an undergraduate. If he had not been a small degree civilized, he very probably would not have troubled him-self with boots at all; but then, if he had`

```
not been still a savage, he never would
have dreamt of getting under the bed to
put them on. At last, he emerged with his
hat very much dented and crushed down over
his eyes, and began creaking and limping
about the room, as if, not being much
accustomed to boots, his pair of damp,
wrinkled cowhide ones — probably not
made to order either — rather pinched and
tormented him at the first go off of a
bitter cold morning.
```

"Oh, you savage, savage me," Harry says, and there is already a well-hung tent in the middle-class bed. But after that, Harry says, "He's not saying you can't like you say I can't or shouldn't when I wear a frock or a malo, even though Uncle Mel Kalahiki gave me permission for the malo. Poppa is just trying to be kind."

I know.

Poppa just trying to be kind is better than a fist in the face (Sydney 1967, 1968, 1977). Better than your head banged up against the wall in your bedroom by some guy who just fucked you and now feels anxious about fucking you (Sydney 1975 Colombo 1982 Baltimore 2002) Better than Fairy saying, "I am excited to see the boy inside you. Let him out so we can play." (Beijing 2010) Better than this type of condescension: "Everybody knows you're really a man, but we let you work here anyway because you're so beautiful." Better than a law against it. Better than: "Why in heaven's name would any sane person want to do things like that to their body. And the people who help them, well," my mother says from deep sunk into her new recliner chair and watching some television report about Anthony Loffredo in France who is becoming what he calls "a black alien" and has had his nose and upper lip removed, his tongue forked, and his body and his eyeballs tattooed black. "What an unkind thing to do to his poor mother."

People are kind of kind about people becoming above their station, middle-class, rich, powerful. These days more people are more kind than not about becoming across sex and gender. But kindness is rare for people becoming aliens of any hue, for people becoming rain, a cloud, even a neon light, people becoming tabby cats and Scottish folds, people becoming Dalmatian dogs, those lovely, lovely spots. People becoming bats, Sumatran tigers, lions, coyotes, dragons, lizards. Crazy, sick, mad, freak, looney, nutter, whack job, sicko, people say of people who become non-human animals. Yet, like humans becoming across sex and gender borders, humans becoming cat, dog, lion, eagle, you name it, occurs in many cultures and many histories. In Maya culture, I have read, the human being is always at least two, human animal and animal, and the human animal becomes animal all the time and the animal becomes human animal all the time; this constant becoming is the order of Maya things: nahual.

I once slept with a Haywards Heath man who wanted to do it again on the condition that I affirm him as an alpha wolf and affirm myself as a beta she-wolf, and he was not speaking in metaphors. I tried not to judge his wolfness or not. Sigmund Freud had failed to relieve Sergei

Konstantinovitch Pankejeff of his conviction that he was a wolf, so who was I to try anything?

•

In *The Metamorphosis*, Gregor Samsa becomes suddenly a giant insect. The consequences of his transformation from man to big bug might be a parable for McKenzie Wark or anybody else with a boy birth certificate becoming woman or any human animal becoming animal, any Frenchman becoming a black alien: Gregor Samsa's family, boss, and coworkers no longer understand him; he loses his ability to earn a living and support his family; his mother faints at the sight of him; his father stones him with apples; the family tries to pretend Gregor doesn't exist, and he dies alone and reviled.

•

Fairy yearns but has trouble with becoming happy partner, iconoclastic intellectual, autonomous woman, cosmopolitan sophisticate, fearless dyke, amazon, in love with me because of who I am rather than despite. She is afraid becoming breaks the rules and brings punishment the way becoming *out* lesbian and a bit butch brought threats of suicide from her mother, the silent treatment from her father, talk of psychiatric treatment, and three men chasing her down silent Ludwigstrasse at eleven pm Fairy just wants to *be* but "There is no me in me," Fairy says in one of those conversations and gouts of tears. She thinks no me in me is a flaw. I want to say perfect or, if not say perfect, say, that is one point of view. I want to tell Fairy she's hit upon a fundamental truth about the human condition, but not all of the truth, not the only truth, and I want to say something about life is short, let yourself into the river of time, but I want to say something about life is short and river of time in a way that is not trite, and I can't, so I say nothing, and I wait until it is too late to say anything except variations upon I hate you and I hate what I've become with you; say how it hurts every time she rolls back time to stop the flows of yearning and becoming and takes me with her into that garden where nothing changes after about the age of fourteen.

A psychiatrist had Little Carol committed to the state asylum in 1966 and again in 1970 upon diagnoses of schizophrenia characterized by delusions of being and/or becoming a woman. Her treatment consisted of learning to knit beanies, doses of chlorpromazine (white pills one or two or three), fluphenazine decanoate (injectable suspended in sesame oil very ouch once every two weeks or so), haloperidol (daily pink too many side effects), trifluoperazine (blue but ataxia). Yet Little Carol would not relinquish her woman. Her doctors and all but one of the nurses could not relinquish their conviction that biology is truth, and there it was again: you'd have to be mad to think yourself a woman when biology says otherwise.

※

Sometimes, McKenzie Wark posts pictures of herself as boy and man on Facebook.

Worthy of the Event

What does she intend?

I've done a pretty good job of becoming woman, becoming middle-class, becoming intellectual, becoming in the world, becoming sophisticated, well-read, calm, wiser, becoming old, yet, there does seem to be a me always and unchangeably what and who I was at the time of those first bawls in the delivery room, or if not that far back, there might be a me still with me now and begun at the time of my father's sudden and early death. There might be a structure of feelings, an unaltered and sometimes unbecoming inner colloquy about how I am to be in the world and how I am to make my world for me.

I am not McKenzie Wark nor becoming McKenzie Wark. I am not the sort of transsexual woman who posts pictures of herself from before my woman got underway. I have four pictures of myself then: three Kodak Box Brownie snapshots in which I am two years old and in my mother's arms, five years old and crying, seven and spick-and-span for a day in town, and, if you know my dead name and where and when I went to high school and want to see gorgeous, there I am, sixteen and about to break out of *everything*, including what it says on my birth certificate, no matter the cost. I do not show these pictures of before. I have become too far beyond them and then. I am not in them except for something almost phylogenetic in the fearless, probing, tender, and terrified gaze of that gorgeous sixteen-year-old about to take off then.

I once showed that gorgeous sixteen-year-old about to take off then to a.k.a. Victor Mature who said, "What high school was that?" and went back to his study of the lyric poems of Sappho. Harry said, "Sexy," and tried to finger me. Fairy burst into tears because she thought she'd missed out on something. BamBam said, "Were you a dyke in high school?"

Privilege is what I see when I see McKenzie Wark's pictures of herself *in the guise of* boy and man. I see how what she had before becoming McKenzie Wark endures now. I see the white man networks, resumé, resources, right to speak, and confidence that white men of any class acquire and develop when they *do* white man long enough. I see that privilege kept for life. I see privilege perhaps diluted, but not lost, not given up, when white-man-doing-white-man becomes white woman. The economist, Deirdre McClosky, for example, suffered much while becoming woman at the age of fifty-three but had money in the bank, professional status, and networks which endured through her becoming woman sufficient for her to renew and develop her career and wealth. McKenzie Wark's becoming woman has lost her things, that's for sure; it might have hurt and made joy in equal measure, but she has not lost the privilege to speak and be heard. McKenzie Wark has not lost her professional networks, not her job, not the space in discourse she made for herself before becoming woman. Just the opposite. McKenzie Wark has used her becoming woman to expand the reach of her voice, to refresh her writing and create new opportunities for herself. Her becoming woman is a marketing tool for her ideas. She has successfully commodified her becoming woman. Trans is her new brand.

"You are just envious. You are sour grapes," Norma Mapagu says. "Try to be better than yourself. Maybe McKenzie Wark's boy and man pictures on Facebook are evidence of some enduring and stable being within all her becoming."

"You can't say that," I say.

"And covetous is a sin," Norma Mapagu says. "Divisive." And Norma Mapagu says, "Also, I worry. It's like you're stalking McKenzie Wark."

I say, "It's not possible to stalk a *brand*, is it? And, anyway, you know I don't get the hots for girls in dresses."

✸

If Friedrich Nietzsche's current address is c/o the black star upon which clever beasts invented knowing, I will visit him there where he is immortal and shares an office with Gilles Deleuze, takes a latte with Maria Callas, and, look, that is David Bowie at the next table in a ghostly restaurant, and Lili Elbe off in her phantasmic studio painting clever beasts in oils. I want to hear what Friedrich Nietzsche may have to say when I tell him about McKenzie Wark's boy/man pictures. I will say: "Could you have been wrong in *Twilight of the Idols* to say that intrinsic, stable being is an empty illusion, that we have only incessant and myriad becoming? I mean, Herr Professor Doktor, I understand your purpose when you wrote *Twilight of the Idols* was to rip apart the values of fin de siècle Europe. You wanted to blow religiosity out of the water. You wanted to poke Socratic reasoning in the eye, break up Parmenides' all-is-one argument, have a go at mechanistic thinking and industrialization and the scientific arguments about how the size of your cranium, the shape of your mandible, the length of your femurs and tibia, the colors of your skin, a penis, decide who you are. I get that, but now, here, where we are, and late nineteenth-century Europe far behind you, were you wrong to insist becoming is all there is?"

I expect Friedrich Nietzsche will have become laconic on the black star. He will say the German equivalent of humbug, which is humbug: "Humbug," and, "*I* am not here, neither are *you*."

And I might say: "Your idea of endless becoming is like Leon Trotsky's theory of permanent revolution, and we know how that turned out."

Friedrich Nietzsche won't be having it: "Do we?"

I say, "In Josef Stalin and a hail of bullets in Coyoacán."

Norma Mapagu butts in, "Even on a black star, you can't get it that wrong. It was an ice-axe."

Friedrich Nietzsche shrugs. Ice axe or machine gun, who cares. So dismissive, he is, of the facts, of what he has not experienced.

I say, "Something of us is here. It is pointless to dismiss that. I know *you* are here after all, Herr Professor Doktor. You know I am here. In some way, some form."

Friedrich Nietzsche says: "We are not men of knowledge with respect to ourselves."

To this dismissal I offer Adrian Bejan's constructal law governing flow systems: "Vascular forms," I say to Friedrich

Nietzsche wherever we are, "persist across time through their own evolution, for example, trees, the human venous flow system especially capillaries, river deltas, the vascular form of the Spark data management system. From Bejan, we can infer that fundamental patterns, in addition to the delta pattern, can *be* in a stable and intrinsic way across time and space. Thus, something fundamentally you and something fundamentally me may be always present in and of us even when *we* are not."

Friedrich Nietzsche says: "Humbug delta anything, and you, you are in error. You under-read me. I have never said there is nought but becoming; I have said that being is becoming. Reflect, if you please, upon Hegel's lesson, the mouse which ate a consecrated communion wafer."

And with that, Friedrich Nietzsche stalks off in search of Gilles Deleuze. His ectoplasmic mustaches curl like smoke. He gnashes his teeth and says over and over again as he goes into the sidereal ether, "*Time time time time time time.*"

For time is the venue for every becoming. Being may occur outside of time but becoming cannot happen without time. Some may say, becoming is time. Death may be the ultimate becoming/time conjunction beyond which, as far as I know, becoming, being, and time itself are completed, finished, and done with for each human being and maybe for other animals, even trees and begonias. In that church on Coleman Street in the town where I grew up, death was the final human becoming into a time without time, a form without form, within which – no one knows the hour nor the day – the Messiah would come again and some part of my being not finished by death nor rotted away and turned to dust would be reactivated, *if righteous*, transformed into an eternal being which might or might not take a human form, no more becomings, ever.

Until I thought about what eternity in a holy city built of bling listening to Jesus Christ dispense beatitudes forever might really be like, the Coleman Street church version of death seemed like a blessed becoming. I said as much to the devout principal of my school. He had the habit of sticking his hands in his pockets and juggling his testicles while teaching square roots or the climate of New Zealand or the wars and rumors of wars and the Whore of Babylon, but at this, he stilled his balls and said, "God does not want us to look forward to death but to His promise for the righteous in the thereafter."

And on Thursday night, the principal, his balls, and Pastor Bullock came to the screen door of the house for a chat with my mother, who held the door tight shut and spoke through the screen: "There is nothing wrong with my child. Mind your own business. And in my opinion, you should be rewarding any child who looks forward to eternal life in the presence of Our Savior, sort of thing. Thank you."

✵

The first Qin emperor, Qin Shu Huang, yearned for eternal life. He wanted to become immortal so that he could *be* forever, liberated from time itself and become one hundred percent being. Qin Shu Huang was the first of many to swallow the Pill of Immortality, drink elixirs of gold and precious stones, especially jade, sip on mercury painstakingly refined from cinnabar, munch purple boletus flowers, refuse to eat cereals, try to stop breathing, and have their orifices plugged to stop life from leaking away.

They wanted to stay, their `lives and flesh like ice and snow`. Lives without time, without becoming, eternal beings, they `walked through the raging fire and were not burned; stepping lightly, they crossed gloomy torrents; they flew in the pure air, with the wind as harness and the clouds as chariots, they enlarged their boundaries to include all of space and went where they will`.

Qin Shu Huang's dream of immortality was more (or less) than a dream of life abiding forever. It was a dream of unchanging home, of liberation from the prison of time, of not wanting, not needing to be somewhere and be someone else. Immortals cannot even die of boredom caused by their eternally stopped being, they just go on and on and on. Immortality deactivates being, makes it inert, so that its possibilities, which are the fuel of becoming, no longer awaken. How unbecoming.

※

Parmenides' poem, *On Nature*, is more than a poem. It is a tool for transformation of the reader and the reader's relationship with the truth and opinion. It is a lesson in critical thinking. It is a tract upon the politics of suspicion: ask why this is this and that is that and who says so. Think twice about categories: that is like, this is unlike, this is being, that is becoming. *On Nature* begins with a lesson on the falsities of binarism. There is no division between life and death, Parmenides reckons, and points to the presence of living beings in Hades, which is not the kind of evidence that works for us these days but was solid data in the Hellenic world in the sixth century BCE. Parmenides calls out and overcomes the false divisions between being and becoming. Nothing is not nothing. Nothing is a part of being. Being is nothing. Yet, for Parmenides, who is the father of the western theory of being (ontology), being is everything. But he does not argue that being is all there is to us.

Parmenides would not say that McKenzie Wark is always and invariably a man no matter how she understands herself, no matter how much estrogen she takes. Parmenides is not telling us that no matter how many consecrated communion wafers Hegel's mouse eats, it remains forever just a mouse. The Parmenidean McKenzie Wark becomes a woman. The Parmenidean Berlin mouse becomes God, for sure. But if you are Parmenides or of a Parmenidean inclination you will argue for some eternal being in all the becoming. You will speak of some permanent *home* anchoring both the becoming-woman of McKenzie Wark and the becoming-God of Hegel's mouse. For Parmenides, all changing forms are but manifestations of a single and eternal being. It feels like it is a twenty-first-century cop-out to say that this single and eternal being for humans is our shared emotional experiences, but I am saying it anyway: where our homesickness leaves us, our forever home, the place for which we yearn is how each of us do and know happiness, do and know anger, do and know want, do and know joy, do and know lust, amusement, envy, grief, fear, confusion, do and know wonder.

※

After the great disasters at Fukushima and other places in northeastern Japan, O's mind begins to float above her body, as high as stratospheric. She was never voluble, but now her talk is scarce, reduced by events and how the events reveal vast, unbearable patterns. On the Nanpu Express from Okayama to Kōchi, we stop at some point in high Shikoku where the mountains have turned to liquid sunshine in the spring rains. O says, "Speaking of being." (We were not but had been the week previous.) She says, "There are times when it may be useful to drop my commitment to what can be seen and focus instead on things hidden. I am becoming like that old Honda in the last moments of the last of Mishima Yukio's last four novels. Giving up after a lifetime of trying to make things visible."

I am surprised to hear O mention Mishima Yukio. I learned years ago to not speak of him nor his works in front of her, for the one time I said something about

Forbidden Colors, a faint shudder passed across the planes of her face in a way that told me not to mention Mishima Yukio nor his works ever again. I am even more surprised to hear O mention the last of Mishima's last four novels which is generally thought rushed and made shallow by Mishima's haste to get it finished and with his publisher before he and his beautifully-uniformed little militia took over the office of a senior officer and held him hostage at Japan Self Defense Force Camp Ichigaya in central Tokyo, a theatrical act political act calling for return to some imaginary Japanese past and ending in Mishima's seppuku ritual suicide, an agonizing disembowelment with a botched coup de grace be-heading (kaishaku) hack, hack, hack, when is this fucking head going to drop off.

The Nanpu Express winds down the mountains to the Pacific coast. Over food posing as art at La Prima Volta, O talks of Mishima again. She tells me his last four novels explore the Hossō Buddhist sect's philosophy of reincarnation in which human beings have eight forms of consciousness. O says, "Speaking of Parmenides (we were not), this eighth form of consciousness – alaya vijnana – is certainly the single, eternal being of each of us. It is home."

The Hossō sect says our eighth consciousness is what reincarnates. In each life, the eighth consciousness stores the fundamental elements of our lived desires, our aversions, our joys and griefs, our karmic balance sheet. At death, the eighth consciousness travels into a new body already imbued with its own seven other consciousnesses.

Worthy of the Event

"This is impossible to see," O says "And that is what Honda in Mishima's tetralogy fails to learn until it is too late. All that time he spends searching for signs. Baka da, na."

Honda is the unheroic, unattractive un-hero of Mishima's four last novels. In the first, he is young and deep in an intense, unrealized homoerotic relationship with Kiyoaki, who dies aged 20, leaving Satoko, a woman he has seduced, in the lurch and Honda bereft. Kiyoaki's last words to Honda are, "I'll see you again," and in the next three novels, Honda tries to see Kiyoaki seeing him again. He explores the Hossō philosophy of the eighth consciousness and reincarnation, but he (or Mishima) fails to understand the radically intangible form of the eighth consciousness itself. Honda spends his life looking for Kiyoaki's three moles and for Kiyoaki's memories of their time together on the bodies and in the minds of others, especially a narcissistic young ultranationalist, a manipulative Thai princess, and a sadistic young man who abuses Honda cruelly. Nothing about his search for Kiyoaki reincarnated goes well for Honda and he arrives at his old age wondering if there is anything single, anything eternal to human beings, if anything happens at all.

Close to death, Honda visits Satoko (Kiyoaki's ditched lover) who is now the abbess of a Hossō convent near Nara. She does not recognize Honda. She denies any knowledge of Kiyoaki. What Honda had remembered and understood to be true appears to him now as a lie. Has there been no Kiyoaki, ever, no young ultranationalist, no Thai princess, no sadistic young man?

Perhaps then there has been no I, **Honda** says.

That too is as it is in each heart, **the abbess says and takes him to the south garden where** maples dominated the grove beyond the lawn. A wattled gate led to the hills. Some of the maples were red even now in the summer, flames among the green. Steppingstones were scattered easily over the lawn, and wild carnations bloomed shyly among them. In a corner to the left were a well and a water wheel. A celadon stool on the lawn seemed so hot in the sun that it would surely burn anyone who tried to sit on it. Summer clouds ranged their dizzying shoulders over the green hills. It was a bright, quiet garden, without striking features. Like a rosary rubbed between the hands, the shrilling of cicadas held sway. There was no other sound. The garden was empty. He had come, thought Honda, to a place without memories, nothing. The midday sun of summer flowed over the still garden.

THE END

✵

Worthy of the Event

No amount of reading and chewing my cud, no amoint of wanting to know, brings me nearer to certain about what being and becoming are. I am not a philosopher. I cannot let myself fall to either side of the discussion about whether being is all or becoming is everything. All that I have is the opinion that becoming might be a poem, and like a poem, each becoming begins as a lump in the throat, a sense of wrong, a homesickness, a lovesickness, and, if becoming is the poem, being is the element from which the lump in the throat, the homesickness, the underway of us, the poem, is forged.

For this, I have no evidence except the anecdotal: My mother's element, her being, and her poem, was garden. She was a couple of port wine magnolia mulched and fed and reliable with enameled green leaves and swooning blossoms come spring. She was a bed of mignonette lettuce, a row of grosse lisse tomatoes. She was a Japanese maple tree struggling to become beautiful on a therapy of red dirt, pills of sheep shit, and obstinance. She was scornful crab grass, dandelion, and paspalum. She was an uncorralled collation of wonga wonga vine, old man's beard, and dusky coral pea. My mother's human body and her human mind gave less attention to themselves than to the gardens she grew as signs of her true being, and in those gardens, my garden mother and the garden she made to show her being to the world became one. Where's our mother we would say, and our answer never changed: garden. What is our mother, we never said for we didn't want the garden our mother was. We wanted the Mom she was always becoming.

III: nuclear cats

Big Denise's crim boyfriend doesn't like no from you fucking queens so he forces Big Denise, who doesn't do anal because she's keeping penetrative sex until she gets a vagina in Casablanca or Cairo or wherever vaginas can be got in 1967, I don't know, and ten days later, Big Denise can't shit, she has to pull it out with her fingers, and the pain makes Big Denise feel smaller and smaller and tight even though she is still as huge and as soft as usual, and there is blood and creamy pus coming out of her bottom in strings and it is August and the winter winds rake Sydney Harbour with dry fingers so hard and sharp *everything* hurts, and Big Denise gets desperate.

She takes herself off to the emergency room at St. Vincent's where they are, at first, solicitous, yes, Miss, Doctor will see you now, Miss, but when Doctor and Nurse see that Big Denise has not yet been to Cairo or Casablanca or wherever girls went in those days, Doctor says, "Put your clothes back *on*. We don't treat *creatures* like you."

But Big Denise says, "I'm bleeding; it hurts."

Nurse says, "This is a *hospital*, dear, we can't help you,"

Big Denise says, "What am I supposed to do, go to a fucking vet."

Worthy of the Event

Doctor smiles like a suitor at Big Denise and he says, "That is not such a bad idea. I could give you a referral asking him to put you down," and he looks away from himself, Doctor does.

Big Denise says, "If I want euthanasia, I can ask for it myself, and you can stop ogling my tits. I know you want me, you fuckwit, live in hope."

✳

Human beings have their own theories, and it is always amusing to hear them talk about us. Such ignorance and self-assurance!

R. K. Nayaran's speaking tiger does not speak. His is the prevailing condition of animals in human discourse: the beast is dumb and requires ventriloquy to be heard. But putting words into the mouths of animals inflicts upon both animal and human being what Gilles Deleuze would say is the indignity of speaking for others. There exists a whole animal rights activist front of expert ventriloquists created around giving voice to the voiceless and committed to daily administration of the Deleuzian indignity. They charitably ventriloquize what pigs bred for ham *feel* about it and what chickens living in concentration camps from where they arrive on your plate as chicken Kiev, green curry of chicken, or KFC (not on a plate) *agonize* over – there are ten thousand ways of doing chicken – and what pit bulls with their ears cut off and taught to hate *want* or do not want from human beings, and then the ventriloquists convince us that animals cannot speak and that the undignified and undignifying human ventriloquy of animals is an accurate translation of what even silent animals want human beings to know, and designed to bring dignity to animal lives. The ventriloquists foreclose the possibility that if you shut the fuck up and attend carefully to an animal, it might become apparent that animals are not dumb and might not need you to say things like: If I were a cow, the sale of my calf down the river to the meat packing plant would break my heart. Listen to the poor mother bellow: that is heartbroken.

✻

Gertrude Stein thought money is what separates human brains from the brains of other animals – I have ten thousand dollars and know its value; the cat does not – but language is the crux of difference, I have read, I think it was in something by that nineteenth century German philologist, Heymann Steinthal, who thought that human language has almost mystical origins and arrived upon us when some overflow of `soul force` changed into words in the prelinguistic stage of human ascent, and, apparently, animals lack the kind of magnanimous soul necessary for forces to well up and spill out and turn into grammar and vocabulary.

✻

Worthy of the Event

I live with an eleven-year-old blue Burmese tomcat. I *own* him, I am not shy about saying that. He is castrated. We share things: I play Isaac Hayes on the stereo and pick the cat up and dance figure eights and pelvic gyration around the living room with him. This cat was abandoned three times before I found him in a shelter. He is obsessively clingy; he might have been obsessively clingy before, for all I know, and that would explain his history of couch surfing. This cat has vocal outbursts when I leave the house, and, on a bad day, he has outbursts even when I leave the bedroom, not words but enunciations, an arpeggio of strident chords ascending and getting louder on the way up, then down again and quieter, quieter, peep peep, until silent: don't go where are you why are you not here come back I need you deserter return to me get back here I love you bitch you'd better appear get here quick smart or something bad will happen, oh, why don't you obey deserter oh, please you're disappearing there's a bird here's the bed electric heat pad tuna chunks in gravy I don't mind this Science Diet I'm better off without you anyway who needs deserters (sleeping). I decode and *ventriloquize* these cat sounds using a key that always turns high-pitched keens and wails into what they generally mean when they issue from human mouths: distress, and yet, for all I know, that yowling, that screeching could be telling the world, look at me, She's going, and I will be autonomous, the world mine, the whole place to myself, food in the bowl, views of birds and possums running on the roof, and unlimited data to myself.

The deeper the marks upon your subjectivity, the closer to the human conception of animal you go and the more your language, your *representation*, is handled by others. I worked once in a hospital ward for men with catastrophic intellectual disabilities. Don't ask me to repeat what we called them and thought it was fine. We hosed the men down pro re nata, and as needed was often because the men fouled themselves often, and when the naked men grimaced and howled beneath founts of tepid water, we said things like, oh, they think they're at Waikiki Beach, they love it, oh, they're asking where's the Cussons English Leather soap, what fun, Damian, do you want a surfboard? To be honest, it looked like agony to me, but the others said no, no, that's pleasure, you're new to this, you'll get the hang of what they're telling you soon enough, it's not complicated.

•

A friend who is not trans anything that I know of takes to rebutting transphobic posts on Facebook. He explains the principles of transsexual transition, he explains transsexual politics, he explains what transsexual people want. He exposes himself to trolling and the basest sorts of vituperation. It is impossible to not admire my friend's willingness to speak against the demons, to bear it; your heart is in exactly the right place, I think, but I want him to *shut the fuck up*. His explanations are not wrong, yet they are the type of speaking that leaves *me* feeling *de-voiced*, and I am not used to it. I don't need translation. I don't need representation. Get your hands off my strings. I find myself keeping company both distant and proximate with the milk cow you say is grieving the abduction of her calf, with the men in Ward 14 you say love the blasting water, with every answer ever to `What does woman want`, with the sick cat, of whom I say to the veterinarian, she's suffering, it's time, she's ready, with every poor or low income person affected by policies designed and enacted by men and women who've never known a moment of not-enough-money-for-dinner and forget-the-electricity-bill, with my widowed mother who was fired from her job as a nurse's aide because "we know you want to be at home raising your children". The claim to know is more powerful than what you do know. I comment on Facebook: Consider the cow.

My friend replies: Too cryptic.

Listen, I reply, mooooooo.

•

Daisy Gawoon Utemorrah's Dreaming story from Worrorra country up on the northwest coast of the continent now called Australia: The Dilangarri people are dog people who live with gigantic magical dogs. On the days when Dilangarri adults go out to hunt kangaroo or flightless birds as large as stallions and to gather yam, they leave their children and the giant dogs together, saying to the kids, this is a warning, never tickle the dogs and make them laugh because if the dogs laugh, they will speak, and then there will be trouble, but the children *do* tickle the gigantic dogs and the dogs *do* laugh and the dogs talk as it was said they certainly would talk, and as soon as the gigantic dogs speak, all the Dilangarri human beings vanish forever beneath the ground. No wonder we refuse to let animals speak for themselves.

⁂

Mother (at the kitchen table): That magpie wants minced meat.

Me (eating a fried egg): I understand hamburger meat kills native Australian birds.

Mother (indignant): Those magpies never mentioned that to me.

⁂

There I am in court on a hot day wearing a chrome-yellow sundress and a tan and big blonde hair. Magistrate Cocks says, "Blah blah blah blah you are absurd blah blah coming into my court like that blah blah blah get out and get another court date and come back in something blah blah blah."

What I hear is too much skin and spaghetti straps. What I wonder is if chrome yellow might be too strong for a legal proceeding, so when I appear again before Magistrate Cocks, I am in a Merivale dress in terracotta crepe with sleeves, discreet, not skin, pantyhose, and high heels, very nice. It is January 1969 and Magistrate Cocks is unpropitiated by earth tones and demure: "Your blah blah blahsurdity blah blah in contempt blah blah blah blah blah blah." He eyes me up and down like the men hankering for a blowjob or something more eye me up and down on Liverpool Street in the nights, is she worth it, or is *it* worth she, or is it worth it. Magistrate Cocks is not different in my mind except for the lustful car there and the juridical wig here, blah blah blah suck it and blah blah blah blah obtain a new hearing date.

June comes and the Sydney version of winter, and there I am again, but this time, pink bell-bottom pants, a red velvet Nehru jacket, and a Biba floral blouse with a pussy bow picked up just for the occasion at a used clothing store on Downing Street near the court, magenta and some chrome yellow again in it. "Clashing is gorgeous, darling," Big Denise says.

There are six to be tried with me: offensive behavior, soliciting, loitering, consorting, indecent behavior, shoplifting. All rise. Even before Magistrate Cocks sits, he gives me stink eye. He gets his arse in place, and we all sit, and Magistrate Cocks points at me and speaks so clipped and hard, tight edges, there's a period after every word and what he has to say comes out of Magistrate Cocks's cubist mouth in bold, **blah. Blah. Blah. Blah. Blah. Blah. Blah. Blah. Blah.** and *absurd.* **Get a new court date and. Blah. Blah** at me.

I get the feeling that Magistrate Cocks has the feeling I am doing something he doesn't care for much, but *what* I *am* doing wrong according to Magistrate Cocks, that is the ten-thousand-dollar question, it is inscrutable. I am not deaf. I hear every word. I understand absurd and new court date and you and your and and. The rest of it, though, might be Dumi or Hebrew or Armenian or I've got a screw loose somewhere between tympanic membrane and auditory cortex. Even as willing to get it as I am to get it, I can't get it. I am willing like any good Spot, Daisy or Cooper is willing to get human commands to sit, roll over, stay, and tries everything to oblige, without success, until some human system of punishment or reward kicks in, and at last, oh, *that* is what the ruling class wants, and will I do it. "His Honour wants you to come to court in men's clothes," the clerk of the court says, "You're not really trying. You'll end up in the prison out at Long Bay where you can expect a lot of attention."

What attention in the prison out at Long Bay means, I *do* understand, and I *will* obey, but, well, no, I won't roll over and let you think I am all yours and not all mine, Mr. Magistrate Cocks, Your Honour, Your Worship, Your Majesty, no, I will not be Daisy or even Fido. I will be that cat who will have it both ways; that cat who ignores the sound of your cubical voice and waves a tail indolent or smooches your leg and goes around what you want until you give up and say, indulgently, *cats*.

Look at me: I'm in one of Mitchell's navy-blue suits, very tight on me, for Mitchell is a bit smaller. I'm wearing a white button-down shirt and a pale blue tie and lace-up men's shoes with dangerously pointed toes. I'm in big blonde hair looped back and up tight in a knot, and Mary Quant Titch silver beige fingernails, and Andrea false eyelashes made of *real* mink drop-dead on my eyes, and eyeliner everywhere eye-related and somewhat beyond, and Revlon Nothing Frosted on my lips, and not for the first time nor the last I think men's clothes are better than women's clothes, and Mitchell clearly thinks so too (don't touch me, this is serious), and I might wear a suit and tie more often if people don't think it's queer. I'm doing something catty with the court, it might go badly, I don't care, I won't abject myself, but I take a blue Valium before, just to be sure, but Magistrate Cocks must be fed up with me or hungover or over it or he finally sees who I am or he thinks I've *heard* him sufficiently, for he does not use *absurd*, and he does not give me orders I do not understand. He levies a fine of fifty-five dollars, thirty days to pay, but I don't pay, ever. I spend my money on drinks at Bottoms Up Bar and on more drinks for dancing at Chez Ivy and on cat food and a cat toy and the adoption fee for a black kitten with nuclear eyes who moves away after three weeks. Even though I beg him to **stay with me**, the black kitten with nuclear eyes doesn't hear the urgent tones, let alone the meaning of **don't leave me.**

✺

The northern hills and the saffron tiles atop The Pavilion of Buddha's Fragrance jump a few frames. The room shudders. There is a thump, a little thump and groan, but enough to raise people from their seats, ready to run, torpid no more, engaged at last, they are, but not with me nor with Michel Foucault's ways with history. Everybody fingers their phones: Where was that.

More than eighteen thousand people perished, most in the tsunami which came with waves as high as a six-story building and fell upon the land like The End. Walls of water turned to solids, towering in and thickening all the way, a bedlam of ocean, human and animal bodies, hand tractors with their ploughing blades still attached and spinning in the wave, Toshiba washing machines, Mitsubishi refrigerators, SONY flat-screen televisions, beds, dining-room tables, mini trucks, Honda Fits, Nissan Notes, a candy-pink Daihatsu Taft, a black taxi with its driver and passenger still inside and their teeth already knocked out, dinghies and whole fishing trawlers, most of a Lawson Station convenience store, the entire service area of an Esso gas station, seven houses dis-aggregating, and that entire line of black pines from the promenade, many school children, and tens of thousands of dogs and cats and Angora rabbits and gerbils and ferrets and mice and spiders all coming for you, and the temple coming for you, blocking the sky before it gets you running away and batters you to death and leaves you a corpse in a tree or sucks you back out into the ocean or buries you in a crypt of mud, oh, will we ever find Akira-chan?

The Fukushima-Daiichi nuclear power plant melted down and more than two hundred thousand people had to be taken away from showers of radioactive isotopes. The abandoned towns and villages began to ring with the enunciations of animals alive, abandoned, and trying to say something; nights of meows, moos, bleats, howling, chirping, and grunts, mostly unheard, perhaps misunderstood if heard, and then fading as the animals starved to death or died of radiation disease or diseases caused by radiation or were hunted down and executed, perhaps twenty thousand dogs and cats, three thousand four hundred cows, six hundred and thirty thousand chickens, and thirty-one thousand pigs, although some pigs and cows and chickens and dogs and cats, even an emu, went feral and haunted the human world at Fukushima for years, patrolling the magical cedar forests and wooded valleys and the coppices above the steep little bays, roaming the devastation like nuclear wraiths, their livers, their hearts, their kidneys, and their gonads reconstructed as warehouses done out in alimentary shades of pink and maroon and stuffed with cesium. Even now, if you wake in Iitate at three in the morning during the August week of O-Bon festival, and if you walk into the warm dark and toward the mountain called Notegamiyama, you may come upon ten thousand phosphorescent cats dancing among the pre-dawn trees and pulsing green each time they waltz close to radioisotopes decaying reluctantly in the dark soil.

•

Harry tells me the Windscale nuclear accident in 1957 spewed polonium, cesium 137, xenon, strontium, and other radioisotopes all over the United Kingdom and produced tabby cats mutated to the size of mountain lions, their descendants now stalking Cumbria and Cornwall and remote parts of Scotland, mutilating Herefords and sheep, and terrifying children, but when I google it and find *reliable* accounts of the Beast of Bodmin Moor and the Beast of Buchan, there is no mention of the Windscale nuclear reactor fire nor of nuclear radiation. Instead, it seems the giant and murderous cats glimpsed every few years are not nuclear cats at all, but descendants of pumas released from a private zoo in Plymouth, or they are the grandchildren or great-grandchildren of pumas brought as *pets* to Scotland and later abandoned by pilots of the United States Air Force, or it could all be stories, after all, news has origins in medieval reports of monsters and chimeras sighted, impossible beings stalking the fens, haunting our hearts. Not too long before she died, my mother told me how she had read of Christine Jorgensen's sex change in the *Sunday Mirror* in 1953 and had said to my father, "They're making *that* up, 'Ex-GI Becomes Blonde Beauty', I never. It will be centaurs next."

•

The abandoned nuclear dogs of Chernobyl formed their own societies until a battalion of exterminators moved into the ChZO, one of whom was Yevgeny Samoylov. Mr. Samoylov confessed himself surprised to see the nuclear dogs arrange themselves into three concentric semicircles around the pile of lethalized cow meat and kibble he had set out for them. Closest to the food and alone, the ruler: a large mongrel bitch. Beyond her in a semicircle: blonde and harlequin great Danes; St. Bernards, pink panting tongues out even in the late autumn chill; German shepherds. Terriers and spaniels twenty feet further out. Another twenty feet: dachshunds; miniature French poodles born in Ukraine; motley lapdogs for whom there were to be no more laps, ever.

※

Hello, this is Franz Kafka's ape speaking: `The Zoological Garden is only a new barred cage. If you go there, you're lost.`

•

I'm driving south on M-31, the main highway between Sydney and Melbourne, and it's late at night in winter and it's a nine to ten hour drive and I'm moving fast, wanting to get home and the cat, and I don't like driving at night, wallabies and kangaroos and wombats with nuclear eyes

Worthy of the Event

might run in front and clunk, and a semi-trailer overtakes me, even faster, and it is packed it is stuffed with pigs, ten thousand pigs, some ears flapping out between the slats and bars of the rig in the slipstream like `parsnip-colored` hands waving for help, and I see their eyes shining in the dark and watching me in that knowing way pigs watch everything, there they go, zooooooooom
absolute pig awful
  pig pig pig male
    chauvinist pig
      beastly pig fat pig filthy pig
how boarish
        greedy pig insufferable ignorant pig
      pig irritating pig lucky
        misogynist swine murderous pigs
        patronizing pig drunken
        piggly-wiggly fascist
          swine pigs pig rotten
that driver, his heart is covered in lard
          savage pig self-righteous pig
        selfish little swine pigs pig
          foreign pigs selfish pig self-regarding swine
            stupid pig unbelieving swine mean pig
              unfeeling pig pompous capitalist pig
porca miseria
            old fat pig you
          unscrupulous swine
          fucking lying pig
              ungallant swine untidy pig messy
                so many pigs

`they are not pork` and I know those pigs are going from some factory pig farm in the flat country north of Benalla to some slaughterhouse and meat processing plant more convenient for five million open mouths, and I know, too, that the farmer, if he can be called a farmer when he is a *manufacturer* of pigs, and the abattoir and the transport company deliberately shift the pigs at night because the traffic is lighter and because mothers and fathers and the kids in Hyundai SUVs and grannies and grandpas in their white Camrys and ladies with hearts bleeding pink in black Volvos like me are less likely to be on the road and see the transportation of life to death our appetite for bacon causes and, thus, donate to PETA or call their member of parliament and say things like, I insist you push for it to be kinder, I'm telling you, it could have been a scene out of *Schindler's List* or the unfunny parts of *Life is Beautiful*. Who needs to see that?

•

I've been told that animals manufactured for meat in factory farms using methods analogous to the methods used to make microwave ovens in a kitchen appliance factory take any opportunity to escape from what is a forced labor camp in which your work is to make yourself meat, and no matter how hard you work, the work you do does not make you free, it makes your babies into sausages with fennel and you into something delicious when you can't do babies properly any longer, which is why death might come as an improvement for those animals who never get away.

•

Worthy of the Event

Doctor asks what medications I take, and when I get to estrogen, Doctor checks my date of birth, and seeing I'm only thirty, Doctor asks why, and I tell him why, why not, and Doctor's eyes go pale with scientific speculation or something else less objective, and Doctor rubs his hands together, cannot help himself, so predictable, and Doctor asks me to undress, everything off please, and everything off has become predictable too, and I lie down for a full body examination. I could say why everything off, it's a sore throat and/or no. I could escape, but instead I get naked, and I lie down, and Doctor examines me, look at this, oh, look at this, these are creamy and soft, and what do I do with Doctor's turnkey eyes, oh, thanks for asking, everything off, and I spread my legs and I open my arms and I show Doctor the full abundance of my beauty and my glamorous complexity. I am a special animal. I am a white peacock. I am narwhal. I am a black bird of paradise. I am coorinna. I am a dire wolf. I am a unicorn. I am a dragon. I am phoenix. I am transsexual woman, I am animal becoming, I am traversal itself, and he can barely breathe, like a tourist at dawn on the Serengeti, he is entranced. I have Doctor where Doctor needs to be: you dancing monkey, dance.

*

"Him took the dog down to the river and shot him, it was the humane thing to do, that dog was no good anymore, no use whatsoever," my mother says.

Him has said many times, "You are no bloody good, no bloody use," and I know it, and I am now concerned Him will take *me* down to where the Marrambidya bends around the town and Him will shoot *me* there and throw my body into the water where I begin immediately to rot and float, slow, shedding skin and appendages and organs away from Him toward South Australia like the carcass of a dead sheep, like all the pesticide and fertilizer runoff from the wheat and clover grown on stolen land, poisoning the country, but I will be peaceful at last.

•

I don't imagine myself as a dog, ever; they are too eager and "love me, love me, please", is something I will not say, never, not if I live ten thousand years.

•

Miriam Margolyes is a British movie actor with a very nice house in a very nice part of Australia. She finds herself at a loose end after her very nice role in the Harry Potter movies peters out, and she takes a very nice job in an Australian Broadcasting Corporation television documentary in which Miriam Margolyes drives around Australia in a very nice Mercedes Benz mobile home telling everybody she meets, I'm a lesbian. In Darwin, under some unhappy-looking palm trees, she *accosts* a group of transgender or transsexual or sistergirl Tiwi Island women, or at least, it is filmed and edited as accost. "Have you have have you you know had your cocks chopped off yet?" Miriam Margolyes hollers, jocular as a vet casually sexing a chicken except Miriam Margolyes can't help smirking at some private vision of her own outrageousness. Calibrated uncalibrated rudeness is the Miriam Margolyes brand. She seems to admire her capacity to abuse, amusingly, Indigenous trans women who might not exactly be in any position to tell this rich, famous white woman with her phalanx of camera people, *etcetera*, and her nice Mercedes Benz mobile home from the national television network to shut the fuck up white skank and don't speak to me like that.

My own white privilege is of incalculable value yet not valuable enough to keep the same question from me. But my white privilege does mean the question comes at me more courteously put: um, have you, you know, had the operation yet; or something like that. At seventy-something there have been so many operations it's hard to know which one I am meant to answer for. Ask me about the operation again, cunt or cock, when did you, go on, do it, don't be polite, you need to know, I know, ask me and watch me turn into a thing because nobody asks an attack helicopter or a vase or a Toyota anything at all.

※

"Fabian's whippet doesn't like women," Fairy says when Fabian's whippet sidles up to me on the sofa and leans against me with moony eyes but lifts his upper lip, nasty, ready to bite whenever Fairy even looks at me. Does Fabian's whippet smell transsexual on me? Does he sniff out a difference between neovagina and other vagina and make choices about baring doggie teeth and biting or fall in love, kiss me honey, according to neo or not? Or maybe

Fabian's whippet smells the difference between kind and cruel. Is that what it is? I'm confused about gender and the smell of it, and I feel confused about Fabian's whippet, but I am not at all confused about Fairy. I fondle Fabian's whippet's ears and rub between those swooning eyes with my fingertips, tender, and say, "You're a lovely dog, Picasso."

•

Even the windows and climate control in this golden Cadillac, even these golden rings upon my fingers can't keep this smell out. There on the right, west of Bakersfield, ten thousand Black Angus cows and steers undertake their finishing period in the rain. They stand en masse, wet, glossy and quiet, stuffed with fodder and antibiotics and steroids every day until market weight. And the spring rain falling soft, and the shifting of forty thousand cloven hoofs on the mud soft, and the whisper of black bovine hips one upon the other, soft, and somebody snorts softly. They are not talking, they are not telling their stories, they are not citizens, and there is nothing to hear except soft in the Central Valley. Drive on.

•

The vet sticks a long aspiration needle between the ribs of my cat, over and over and over and over and over he sticks it in, trying to strike some reservoir of fluid he calls serous collection and is certain lies in there somewhere between her lungs and her ribcage. Over and over. "She's not Texas," I say. My cat never struggles. She does not cry out. She submits and looks at me, and I wonder if her submission is because she is ill or because she was trained to submit

Worthy of the Event

during the years when her sole justification for life was her ability to bear kittens for sale at a thousand dollars a pop, twice a year or more, ten thousand dollars a year and up, and always a caesarean delivery to make sure no thousand-dollar baby dies. Beneath a veldt of pearly hair, old scars ridge my cat's belly. The vet gives up. He passes her to me. She bites his hand as she goes, hard, and he says "Ow" and tiny cabochons of blood appear, and the vet nurse says, "Cranky thing."

•

I saw dogs flirting, tongues hanging out happy every which way. After flirtation, the dogs fucked and I burst into tears. Aunty Snow was, as ever, worthy of the event. "Don't let it upset you," she said. "This is just something automatic. You will be surprised." And I was surprised but never automatic, and it was not the doggie copulation making me cry. All that dog longing brought the tears, all that grinning with lolling pink, wet tongues and those dancing bodies, do you like me, I like you, do you want to love me, let me love you, do you want to do it with me seemed like a choreography of yearning and permission to me, and I cried because would anybody ever dance longingly for me like that, or will it always be go at me like hungry mouths go at sandwiches, go at me like that young soldier from the base at Kapooka, the one with marble skin and titian hair and the almost blue dick went at me in the swimming-pool change room and said after he rinsed his surprise off my chest, gentle, "Don't be shocked. You're a lovely little boy. A man is an animal," and I thought, I am not shocked, I am surprised, I've *seen* animals, and you are not an animal. I am not a boy.

The cat seemed shocked *and* disgusted the first time I kissed him on the mouth, but I kept doing it and now he puts his face up for it. I suspect the cat of trying to pucker unpuckerable lips. I have read that cats cannot learn through collaboration because `they don't use a collaborative approach, it goes against their motivations,` but I think learning to kiss is always collaboration.

Fairy does me with a large black strap-on. I don't query the color. I don't like to be fucked but sometimes you have to. I don't like plastic or latex or rubber or silicone anything but sometimes you do. I focus on the weekends in Paris or Safranbolu or Munich and dinners in Istanbul restaurants with views of the Sea of Marmara, books we read together, the Greek temple pillars golden in the morning sunshine at Agrigento, a sandwich in Berlin in winter. Taking the large black strap-on is called *accommodation*, like a Motel 6, we leave the light on for you and please come again. I am not quoting. When it happens, which is not that often, I wonder if Fairy will notice I am tepid, my light is not really on, and I wonder, too, if how I feel about the black strap-on is how the cat feels about being kissed and neither of us can say so, no.

※

Angelina started spinning in the water, turning, turning, so graceful it looked, as though the fish had perfected a dance routine for me. But then Angelina's spinning went on, unceasing turning into the night, and her eyes fixed on me pleading, it seemed, as she whirled around around around around, ten thousand watery pirouettes staggering and imperfect until dawn came up on knives of light and I knew it meant killing even though Angelina was unstintingly loyal, always came to the glass for me as soon as she saw me enter the room, and how beautiful you are, Angelina, even now, on the edge of The End, like a gold-and-ebony brooch shimmering in the aqueous shadows.

But that spinning.

I took the softest net and scooped Angelina from the tank. I held Angelina in my hands soft and rested her soft on the white marble cutting board, one eye up and a little panicked. I took up that large Japanese kitchen knife I had made Harry buy for me, and I chopped Angelina's head off hard at a point which I estimated might be the right point and that was that, although for a few seconds, with her head separated from her body, Angelina's mouth still moved like talking and her upward-facing eye drank me in, Mary Queen of Scots in one of those movies came to mind, but she was just gasping for water and then she went. I diced Angelina's body into almost perfect tiny cubes and fed them to the neighbor's cat. "Angelina understood that only life matters," I said to Harry, who had aghast lips at me and, like most human beings, was ever afraid of dying in one way or another and performed complex but unacknowledged routines for avoiding The End of anything.

"But she was your pet," he said.

Harry always preferred the obvious.

It is not dying, nor even the manner of dying so much, that causes the suffering of sufferers, human beings and other animals. It is life and the conditions of living that hurt and misshape all living beings, some more than others. Angelina had been as comfortable as any cichlid could be in a tank and not some Amazonian tributary. It was a good, big tank, and clean, and little forests of healthy plants, and I catered to her hunting desires with live dinners twice a week, oh, how Angelina loved that and her ruthless harvest of bloodworms who knew she was coming and writhed in anticipation. Angelina was fairly happy in it, I think, I told anybody who asked, happy, except when the Kona weather stopped the trade winds, filling the air with the color of volcano, and the temperature went up very high, and I threw ice cubes into her home to keep her water cool enough and it was clear Angelina did not care for *that*, pursing those fish lips at me, this is not a cocktail.

•

We use *which* and *it* on things, on animals we need to be machines, and on animals we plan to turn into things: meatballs; a handbag; an IVF procedure; a mitral valve. She, he, and who come into play only when human beings see themselves or some vision of the human condition in the animal. Then we *care*. The walls between pronouns for things, pronouns for people, and pronouns for things in which we think we see qualities we have decided are human qualities, leak badly, they are perforated. Don't care and do care, human, thing, animal, *he*, *she*, *who*, *it*, and *that* flow back and forth so quick and so mutable animals must find humans confusing. In Isaac Bashevis Singer's *The Key*, the widow Bessie Popkin comes upon a black street cat. She hates *it*. *It* sniffs Bessie's bag. *It* rubs its back on Bessie's leg. *It* hooks its tail and speaks, and very quickly, Bessie wishes she could give *her* something to eat. Bessie is lost on the street and tired and hungry herself; the cat might wish *she* could give Bessie something to eat but if *she* does, it will not be said that the cat *cares* for Bessie; it will be said that the cat wants Bessie to learn how to hunt.

※

This is a time when human beings consume so many animals that sheep, chickens, cows, pigs, turkeys, ducks, goats, salmon, shrimp, quail, and geese must be grown and harvested like crops of rice or wheat, en masse, cut like broccoli for the table, must be cropped for the clothes we wear, those heavenly pillows, the sofas upon which we sit, and for the medical treatments that allow us to have babies or not and survive cancer or not. My favorite Sergio Rossi shoes used to moo. This is a time when millions watch crush videos in which women wearing underwear or negligee, stiletto heels or bare feet, stomp and pierce rabbits, cats, small dogs, mice, ferrets to death, suffocate them with cling wrap, vivisect them with kitchen knives, see me drown a kitten in extra virgin olive oil, watch me pierce a rabbit's cranium with an ice pick, bludgeon a rat. Jerk off while you watch, go on, do it.

This is also a time when many people obsess about animals as feeling beings and as objects of welfare, agonize and coo over them, wonder about their subjectivity or not, perv endlessly at them, and weep on their screens at what they are told is animal unhappiness. Some people grin and chuckle and share, all happy and *moved* at animal antics and animal salvations, Grumpy Cat (RIP), animal rescues, animal tricks, animal adoptions, ducks making friends with tigers, clever animals, a welter of living animals amid mass animal exterminations and rashes of animal gulags where the only forms of labor are to bear more animals and to transubstantiate into a commodity.

·

When my cat is stuck in one of his pacing fits, caused, I think, by a life lived unnaturally indoors, the best remedy is high-definition videos of squirrels and chickadees and blue jays eating seeds from a feeder in the snow somewhere in the Green Mountains of Vermont or the Connecticut River Valley, and while my cat watches his shows, which he does intently, I cook and eat a lamb cutlet or a chicken thigh in Australia, perpetually trapped somewhere between two countries and between turning animals into human beings and turning animals into food. "You would become food for *him*," Fairy says, "if necessary. Now let *me* eat you." Our discrepant ways of talking and thinking and being about animals are a late modern agonistic: wanting to consume but fearing that consumption may not be quite the right thing.

✳

```
Miss Blanche, having given through her
tears a complete account of this event,
```

```
assured me that, to maintain our own
parental love and to enjoy our beautiful
family life, we, the cat-race, must engage
in total war upon all humans. We have no
choice but to exterminate them. I think
it is a very reasonable proposition.
```

•

In every human brain there might be some dendron secreting human fear of some animal retaliation for how we've managed interspecies affairs (*The Birds*), but nobody believes that Natsume Sōseki's cat really talks. There is not that much magic in the world. Mrs. Nakamura says, "In some back-block parts of Japan there are some people who think all animals talk. Some of them even think, even now, that Namazu might cause earthquakes."

I say, "Really."

Namazu is a catfish the size of Tokyo. It is usually kept under tight control by a humanoid deity of the Kashima Shrine who presses the foundations of the great shrine down on Namazu until the metropolis-sized catfish cannot move. Or sometimes, in some accounts, some less celestial fellow uses a gourd to the same effect: no movement equals no earthquake. Sometimes the Kashima deity or the guy with the gourd falls down on the job, looks the other way, dozes off, and as soon as the weight of the shrine foundations or the pressure of the gourd eases off, the city-sized catfish thrashes around, causing the earth to shudder and quake. Mrs. Nakamura says, "Long before the ground begins to shake, the cats get the feeling that the great shining deity has lost its focus and Namazu is now able to move. They feel what is coming. That is cats. The cats feel everything but know nothing. People, on the other hand. Well, what is knowing but a feeling?"

I am unsure of all of this, but my relationship with Mrs. Nakamura does not permit open disagreement or even questions.

※

René Descartes, or you may blame Plato, thought animals were machines incapable of intention and adapted response. Animal behavior is automatism: your cat is an algorithm. The only animal endowed with subjectivity is you.

Animals themselves object to this proposition. Look animal conduct. If, in looking, you refuse to arrive at the parsimonious conclusion that what you are looking at can always be reduced to a learned response or to the automated conduct of an algorithm, you come upon the objection of the animal mind, which begins with intention. The mammologist George Schaller thinks that lions, at least, have a sense of history and base leonine action in the present upon what they know about the past. In the Masai lands straddling the border between Tanzania and Kenya, George Schaller observes a lion previously expelled from a pride for killing a cub. When the lion attempts to return to the pride two years after the crime, he is met with refusal and outright hostility from all who witnessed what occurred. He is kept out, too, by those who were not there for the crime itself but who appear to have been *told* about it. Or they do what the elders of the pride who *do* remember tell them to do. Whales clear out once the news of human predation reaches them, and it is clear they *have* been told. Woodpeckers shorten and smooth out twigs until the twig suits an intention, and it is likely that, like human beings, woodpeckers have some category of twig in their minds and a kind of taxonomy of twig sizes and uses.

Animals living in close relationship to human beings frequently demonstrate an intention to resist the relationship or to modify it. Aunty Snow's cows refused to give milk or contrived to poop in their milk if they felt disrespected, called in too early or too late, inadequately flattered before work began on their teats. The cat comes home with an entire roast chicken, still warm, in her mouth. She deposits it on the kitchen table and for days she refuses to eat anything else until presented with the carcass picked clean, at which time she curls her tail into a question mark and lets me know she intends to eat tuna in aspic tonight. A horse kicks its abusive master to death. Elephants wreck a construction camp set up to build a road through their territory. Laboratory animals move to the back of their cages to avoid the hands of scientists and must be persuaded and forced out. Dogs intervene in domestic arguments between humans. A little Cairn terrier lies down on the end of his leash on a hot day and ignores all pleas to walk Oscar, come on Oscar, and the little dog will not move and must be carried home to the climate control. A cat sits right over your malignant tumor and purrs and lets her body heat onto it until you feel you might live one more day.

I have, however, read that, in an effort to fend off a rival who is not there, robins will attack empty air. What does this robin see? Animal intentionality does not mean animals see and do the world in the same way human beings see and do the world. Animal intentionality does not even mean that lions and milking cows and whales in the North Atlantic and a lab rat and a dog and a cat and robins see and do the world in the same way. Every species of animal appears to have its own ways of seeing and managing things, of being in the world.

•

The Japanese Ministry of the Environment announced that in future disasters, pets and farm animals are to, as much as possible, evacuate with what the ministry called, `their guardians. This announcement does not create rights for animals,` **the ministry said,** `be assured the right is for the guardians only and, in any case, it is not a right but a guideline.` We can't have rights of animal evacuation, said officials of the Japan Veterinary Medical Association, talking about animals and rights together will only cause trouble, by which the vets meant that animal rights talk leads to talk about animals having subjectivity just like you and I have subjectivity, opens up the possibility that we all, from flea to me, experience, observe, use, and evaluate relationships and objects to create the world in which we be.

"What about your subjectivity," I say to the retired breeding cat with the pearly coat who has always been able to make *me* feel evaluated and used and loved. She is very sick now, not long to go. She gives me a nuclear eye, which I take to mean, WTF is subjectivity at a time like this, and she sits on my heart and blinks, blink, blink, blink, blink, blink at me and her irises widen and contract like taking ten thousand snapshots to keep for the future.

Worthy of the Event

•

Roberto Marchesini thinks all animals experience, observe, use, and evaluate relationships and objects to create the world. Even insects, who are often the least of animals to us, barely alive, let alone subjective, do it, though not as human beings or many other animals do it, out of stimulus and response. Instead, insects create the world through unconscious mappings of connections, which they manage flexibly so that the map can be an environment, a place, a target, or an operative scheme, as required.

I mention insect subjectivity because it is hard to get your head around it and that hard-to-get-your-head-around condition is one of the things shaping how human beings think of and handle animals. Animal subjectivity can't be human subjectivity, and yet, we assess animal subjectivity or not, mostly not, using terms devised for understanding human beings. Liquify the terms, Roberto Marchesini says, and come up with different measurements for different subjectivities:

Care. Before Angelina fell ill with spinning disease, she hatched seventy-seven eggs and then proceeded to eat the infants one by one until I put a stop to it. Harry said, "God, she's eating her children for fuck's sake, are you sure you want to have that kind of creature in the house?" In the numinous streams and warm pools of the Amazon and Orinoco basins and the Guiana Shield, which are the natural homelands of what we call angelfish, Angelina would not have created a world that included eating her own offspring. Wild angelfish are affectionate and attentive carers of their children, but most female angelfish *in captivity* will try to eat their young as eggs or fry, and as they eat, the proper subjectivity of angelfish appears in its absence.

Longing, which is a form of desire, may also be a condition of subjectivity, and, in dogs, also appears in its negation: `The dog that is allowed to go out and might get cut, or get thorns, is happier than a dog that's just shut inside and not allowed to run around and scrap through the bush. When an animal is put in a position where the expression of its desire is blocked or taken away from it, then it starts to visit harm on itself, biting itself, hitting itself against the wall or barrier, licking too much, to the point of giving itself sores.`

Interpretation. My cat must interpret both his phylogenetic identity as feline *and* his identity as my cat. If he now interprets kissing me on the lips as a characteristic of "my cat" but not of being feline, that is because he knows who he is in the world and adjusts the world accordingly.

•

Without animals, human civilization would not exist in the way it now exists; we could not be what we are and certainly not *who* we are. Yet, we have estranged ourselves from the animals who make us. We have fallen in love with combustion and out of love with the reality of the Umwelt, which is that human and nonhuman animals already live and belong *together* in one world, on a single planet, and our shared home casts us all into interaction and exchange within the same frame of reference.

Worthy of the Event

✴

Barry Lopez says that Yupik and Inupiat peoples in Alaska and Inuit people in Canada do not often use collective nouns for species of non-human animals. They prefer not to say things like, `In springtime the caribou move northward towards the coastal plain of the Beaufort Sea to find the first of the spring greens.` They prefer to say what `an individual caribou once did in a particular set of circumstances — in that place, at that time of year, in that type of weather, with these other animals around.`

I try to know every cat and every dog in my short street as themselves. This is hard. I am not good at it. I try to see each of the six crows, five magpies, and seven brush-tailed possums that hang out on my fences, my balconies, and my roof as six, five, seven individuals. I do not often succeed. Two pied currawongs from a local mob raise chicks in the same tree on the corner every year. I know them as each other when they are in the tree on the corner but, if I run into one of them at the supermarket or down by the local wetlands, I know currawong but I do not know currawong well enough to know there is the male currawong who makes a family in the tree on the corner, and do not expect me to individualize the tribes of rainbow lorikeets eating the blossoms on my ornamental gum trees and then flying off toward the river in a screeching vivid cloud.

For one summer a female redback spider lived in one of the empty garden pots. I looked in on her and spoke to her almost every day and by Christmas she had stopped jerking and hunching up and trying to decide whether to scuttle or not in that spider way. She had found a place for me. I never told that female redback spider the (probably apocryphal) story about how I ate one of her kind in the garden across from the beach at Currarong when I was three, then vomited it onto my onesie. My mother looked at the remains of spider abdomen on my chest, still lustrous black, and that single dot of crimson like good jewelry, and the story is that she said, "How on earth did that get there? Did you eat it? You silly thing. Are you trying to turn into a spider? What next? Red-backs are not food, are they Ev," to my father's mother, who was there with marble cake and looking disgusted. "Spiders are not our neighbors, so we don't eat them," my mother added, causing my grandmother to estimate the intelligence of what had been said with a twist of the lips.

"I'm not sure, Rene, that I like the idea of eating the Skeers family any more than I like the idea of eating a redback spider," my father's mother said.

"Oh, you know what I mean, Ev," my mother said. "Spiders are not a part of normal life."

What does that mean?

Before Descartes and his animals-are-automata-and-only-humans-have-consciousness formulation, the Humanists of the early Renaissance did not think animals were human beings, but they *did* think the cosmos itself was an animal; they did think that divine wisdom might come as a dragon, a sphinx, a serpent, or a lamb. Early Renaissance painters put animal heads on three of the Four Evangelists. Pope Alexander VI had his Vatican apartments decorated with pictures showing bull worship; he thought Apis the bull deity was a predecessor of Jesus Christ. To go into the future with animals, we might need to recover a form of totemism not unrelated to this.

Roberto Marchesini advises zoo-mimesis, by which he does not mean some appropriation or impossible human copying of animal being and comportment. What Roberto Marchesini means by zoo-mimesis is *interpretation* of animal function that has the potential to transform one's own human being through reflection.

That Boeing 787 Dreamliner you fly to LAX is a very far downstream human interpretation of bird subjectivity begun by some ancient human who contemplated albatrosses floating above the surf break at Ka'ena Point or swifts doing their whistling aerobatics along the Adriatic cliffs of the Gargano and thought, that could be me; how could that be me? Human bodies in flight are zoo-mimetic performances of the subjectivity of birds that fly, results of human longing to interpret flight for ourselves. No matter how dreary flying can sometimes seem, and how *ordinary*, every time you soar above the clouds, you enact an ancestor's longing to fly, her yearning to transform the range of human being and extend the quality of human identity by doing bird, by doing worthy of the event that is bird.

•

Bron*wyn* announced her intention to enter the Chameleons drag performance talent show that June with a lip-synch of Dionne Warwick singing Burt Bacharach's "A House is Not a Home". These days, a cisgender straight woman doing transsexual work might be called cultural appropriation, and even back then, Big Denise said, sharp, "I'm not being stroppy, Bron*wyn*, but are you trying to take the piss out of us? And don't ask for my eyelashes. And don't ask for my orange-and-black crepe sheath to do it in, and don't whine if everybody laughs at you." Bron*wyn* had her own eyelashes, and when she asked, she asked for Little Carol's silver lamé, which, on the night, made Bron*wyn* look like a plump bratwurst unaccountably sparkling and gesticulating in the spotlight, and, oh, how we loved *that*. A chair is not a chair, we sang. Bron*wyn*'s glittering lips moved about one second behind each of Dionne Warwick's words. "Faster, Bron*wyn*, it's not a fucking funeral hymn," we yelled, and we took another swig of Big Denise's bottle of green ginger wine and we jeered and laughed until the final Still in love with me, yeah. "So very fish, that was," said Big Denise, but when Bron*wyn* came back to our table with the pink sash for Best Effort, oh, how we loved her for doing us, for her trans-mimetic performance. In December, Bron*wyn* married an American corporal she had met at Whisky a Go Go while he was on R&R in Sydney from the war in Vietnam. She moved to Tuba City and took the Navajo name, Haloke, which means *salmon*. "Fish is fish," Big Denise said when the letter came.

•

Yoeme dance deer at Yoem Pueblo.
  In northern Montana the Crow dance crow.

Worthy of the Event

The people of the Russian Republic of Kalmykia still dance hare.

Men dance lion until they become lion in Senegal.

Him watches our rented twenty-three-inch black-and-white television in January 1966, only when school is out for summer my mother says. Him sees Yolngu men near Nhulunbuy dancing kangaroo in far northern Australia. Him says, "Look at them, will you. They're no better than bloody animals," and he uses one of the five words he has for Aboriginal people. The word is a weapon, I know that, but I am just relieved Him is not using one of the six words he has for me. Him gets up and changes the channel to *Gunsmoke*. Oh, Miss Kitty.

I've been told Yolngu men dance kangaroo before they begin the hunt for kangaroo, which is never open slather, that the Yolngu dance is mimesis of the kangaroo body and of *kangaroo culture*, not dancing to become kangaroo in some shamanic way but to summon the intrinsic kangaroo characteristics of Yolngu people into the frame. After dancing, the hunters go out, kill and eat, then wait until the balance has been restored and then they dance once more, and kill and eat again and, if the kangaroo do not like it, if there is drought, too many taken already, we would rather not deal with loss at this time, or they move elsewhere for sweeter grass, the Yolngu wait for the kangaroo to return, and when they do, the men dance kangaroo again.

Norma Mapagu says, Fine. But do kangaroos dance human?

IV: the disappearance of a.k.a. Victor Mature

The *Aguila Azteca* creaks out of Nuevo Laredo at twenty-seven minutes after nine. There is that desert in the night and there is this moon shedding silver from what always looks like a horrified face to me no matter what they say about beautiful or green cheese or rabbit (if you are Japanese), and there is a.k.a. Victor Mature. He and I are sealed into a cama matrimonial. We'd imagined cama matrimonial was for a married couple as the name implies, and perhaps it is, but we are not quite married, and even if we were, it would not be married in *that* way. Cama matrimonial is a sleeping compartment for one sold for two who are either counting their pennies or who imagine becoming *as one* might be beautiful and want it. That does not describe me and a.k.a. Victor Mature. We don't want fusion. Or we want fusion but cannot. The air-conditioning is in and out. Mostly out. There are no shutters or blinds on the double-glazed windows, and each time the train stops (Monterrey, Saltillo, Santiago de Querétaro) people stare in at us, those two, those big pink gringos sweating and contorting themselves away from each other and into a space they don't understand.

a.k.a. Victor Mature is drawn to anything he imagines to be almost lost, me and Sanskrit for example, and he has brought with him, just for the train, an anthology of Greek lyric poetry. He drags it out and reads "Sappho Fragment 16" to me. At first, where some lines and words have gone from Fr. 16 into time or dust or both, a.k.a. Victor Mature puts in `blah blah`, but `blah blah` turns out to be not at all the effect he wants. Maybe a.k.a. Victor Mature thinks `blah blah` gives the impression that the lines missing from "Sappho Fr. 16" might be `blah blah blah` drivel. Maybe a.k.a Victor Mature thinks it is absence, it is empty space that is the mother of invention, not necessity, which has other things to occupy its time. Oh, what is a.k.a. Victor Mature to do? He stops the `blah blah`. He flattens those wide lips. He flares those geometric nostrils just like the *real* Victor Mature in that old Hollywood movie about Samson and Delilah, and in that one called *The Robe*, tightens *his* lips and flares *his* nostrils when faced with temple pillars in Gaza, when tortured by Caligula's minions in Rome. a.k.a. Victor Mature is just like *that* Victor Mature. "You could sing the whole poem and tra-la-la though the missing bits. That's what they did with poetry in Sappho's time," I say.

A year before a.k.a. Victor Mature and I are in a cama matrimonial on the *Aguila Azteca*, Norma Mapagu met a.k.a Victor Mature, who was not yet a.k.a. Victor Mature, and she said, "He looks like Victor Mature, that old Hollywood movie star. You will be sorry."

"Isn't Victor Mature dead," I said, and, because I don't take kindly to warnings, ever, I got a bit savage and said, "I fail to see any resemblance. Get your eyes checked."

But you know how it is when people say things. You know how saying things makes things real. What you might not know is that I have history with the old Hollywood movie star Victor Mature. My mother thought the old Hollywood movie star Victor Mature was just beautiful. She went all soft when she saw him kissing beautiful Gene Tierney in *The Shanghai Gesture*. And, as it turned out, my mother went all soft every time she saw a.k.a Victor Mature, just because she thought he looked so much like Victor Mature that old Hollywood movie star. So, by the time a.k.a. Victor Mature and I are in the cama matrimonial on the *Aguila Azteca* from Nuevo Laredo to Mexico City, I, too, see Hollywood Victor Mature every time I look at a.k.a Victor Mature, yes, that nose, yes, that mouth, those cheekbones, those hooded and drooping eyes, oh, yes, those shoulders out to here. And, yes, Norma Mapagu was right about the resemblance, but, no, Norma Mapagu was not right about the rest: I could be sorry about a.k.a. Victor Mature but I am not. I am not sorry about him or anything.

Ever.

Almost never.

Well, anyway, on the *Aguila Azteca*, a.k.a. Victor Mature isn't interested in historical authenticity. He does not sing "Sappho Fr. 16". He reads the poem again, ponderous from the beginning including the title, which comes out of his mouth in a way that sounds underlined – <u>Sappho Fragment Sixteen</u> – and this time, a.k.a Victor Mature fills the gaps where the words are missing with ellipses, with `dot dot dot`. On each `dot` of each ellipsis, a.k.a. Victor Mature `dot` looks at me that way he does `dot` and he tilts his head, do `dot` you want it, and, as usual, `dot` I can't look away. This is because a.k.a. Victor Mature is beautiful to me and his beauty is more than some beauty assigned to any old face because that any old face sees the beauty in *me* and thereby becomes beautiful in my sight. No, a.k.a. Victor Mature's unalloyed desire for me does not make him beautiful to me. He is an *objectively* beautiful man. There is never disagreement on that. a.k.a. Victor Mature is so beautiful he can handle me like an object. He can touch me everywhere and as often as he likes, and he does, and on the *Aguila Azteca* that night, he is so beautiful, I know letting him go will ache forever, although, to be honest, for reasons that may become clearer, when the let go happens, seven years in the future, letting a.k.a. Victor Mature go turns out to *not* ache forever. But we are not yet at the letting go time, not even near, there in that tiny sleeping compartment on the *Aguila Azteca* in the beautiful night north of Monterrey.

<u>Sappho Fr. 16</u>

```
some say a host of cavalry
is the most beautiful thing upon the dark
    earth
others say infantry, a fleet of ships,
but I say it is whatever a person desires
it is perfectly easy to make this
```

```
understood by everyone: for she who far
surpassed all mankind in beauty,
Helen, left her most noble husband
and went sailing off to Troy with no thought
   at all
for her child or dear parents,
but dot dot dot led her astray dot dot dot
easily dot dot dot
dot dot dot
dot dot dot lightly dot dot dot
reminds me now of Anaktoria,
who is absent
I would rather see her lovely walk
and the radiant sparkle of her face
than Lydian chariots
and infantry in arms
```

There might be five hundred questions one could ask of Fr. 16, almost infinite interpretations, but a.k.a. Victor Mature says, "So Sappho was a lesbian."

I say, "I'm not sure lesbian existed as a category in Archaic Greece."

a.k.a Victor Mature thinks he's too straight to truck with Greek lesbian categories of any period so he says, "How can anybody find armies and weapons and death in battle beautiful? Were Greeks actually into that?"

Some say that Greeks felt so much guilt about the war with Troy, they turned it into a thing of great beauty as a way of forgetting without forgetting or remembering without memory.

I say nothing about that. I *do* tell a.k.a. Victor Mature I am surprised to hear he thinks military stuff is ugly.

He gives me one of his electric-blue STFU looks so I don't ask why *he* pores over pictures of Soviet long-range bombers and fully armed examples of the General Dynamics F-16 in the latest issues of *Flight International*. Nor do I bother raising the matter of the bond between heroic death in war and eternal beauty, still richly extant in our own time. We've both been to the Shrine of Remembrance in Melbourne and Arlington National Cemetery just across the Potomac River, although we've not been to these places together, and even though a.k.a. Victor Mature might admit to the beauty of a fighter jet and a bomber, I imagine he would flare those acute nostrils at any suggestion of beauty in a war memorial. Neither do I talk about heroic civilizations, although I would if I could.

Homer describes beautifully two hundred and forty beautiful heroic deaths in the final weeks of the Trojan War: `Then Telamonian Ajax struck and wounded young Simoesius, Anthemion's son, a healthy boy who had been born beside the streams of the Simoeis when his mother had gone to see her parents' flocks of sheep upon Mount Ida. On the way back down she gave birth by the river. That was why they named him Simoesius. That boy would never pay his loving parents back for taking care of him. His life was short, because the spear of Ajax cut him down. The young man stepped in front, and Ajax` struck his chest by his right nipple, and the bronze pierced through and came out by his shoulder blade. He fell down in the dust, just like a poplar that grows upon a vast expanse of marshland — smooth on its trunk with branches high up top. A chariot maker with a bright iron axe fells it to form the rim around the wheel upon a glorious chariot. The tree lies drying out beside the riverbanks. So Simoesius, Anthemion's son, was killed by Zeus-born Ajax, and it seems to me that Homer's beautiful rendition of beautiful Simoesius's death makes Simoesius worthy of his final event, makes the battle worthy of death.

I've been to where once was Troy and where those beautiful Homeric deaths of men as beautiful as poplar trees occurred. It was beautiful. I went in the summer in the company of Fairy and Helmut and Fabian and Jutta. We wore shorts and got very pink legs and they made clever remarks about giving head in German in the sunshine at the ruins of Troy, which was right on the sea at the time of the beautiful deaths in battle but is now miles inland with long views from the reconstructed ruins across fields bristling with wheat out to the hard shine of the Aegean Sea. We could see all the way up to Çanakkale. We could see all the way over to the peninsula of Gelibolu, which is Kallipolis in Greek: beautiful city. Australians call Gelibolu Gallipoli, and, especially in late April, visit from hotels in Çanakkale to worship the beautiful graves and memories of the thousands of beautiful young men who died in battle there in World War I; heroes, they are, and they are now beautiful for all eternity, oh, lest we forget. Fairy and Helmut and Fabian and Jutta and I stayed at a hotel in Çanakkale and smoked nargile on the roof, but I have never been to Gallipoli itself and not because I object to the beauties of war memorials and cemeteries so much.

•

In Istanbul, Yasemin ordered the windows and French doors of 5.Kat opened to the first truly warm evening of the year, to all the lights down to the sea, to the lights moving on the sea, to the lights glinting on the Asian side. I did shots of rakı with this Australian woman at the bar. She had just attended the annual memorial service at Gallipoli, "My great-grandfather," she said, "served." Memories of memories she did not have made her serious. Sunshine down there in the bright Dardanelles had pinkened her neck, her décolletage, her arms, her feet, and she was now the same color as the roses on the tables and almost drooping, yet she managed to tell me that the war cemetery at Gallipoli and the dawn service for the beautiful Australian dead were the most beautiful things she had ever seen. "There's the Bosporus," I said, pointing, and she said, politely, "Yes, there is that."

•

On the *Aguila Azteca* a.k.a. Victor Mature gives me question-mark eyes. My answer is: "By Sappho's time, those military and hero things were no longer the acme of beauty. Death in battle was no longer the epitome of sublime. Some say even Solon just wanted to die old and in his own bed. To hell with going out young and gorgeous with some arrow in your heel or some sword driven through your head or heart and lungs, liver, like Achilles and Paris and Hector and Simoeisius at Troy. Homeric Greece was another time. Beauty in time is not always the same beauty."

I do confess: the sword, any sword, all swords, katana, scimitar, sabre, dao, Scythian short sword, keris, the Spartan xyele, paramerion, cutlass, rapier, and the sword as synecdoche of war *does* have a kind of deathless beauty to it. Also, that box in Tutankhamen's tomb painted with the young Pharaoh himself gorgeous in an exquisite chariot harrying his enemies is as beautiful as anything I've ever seen, and I feel sure that the men who did the terracotta soldiers at the tomb of the emperor Qin Shu Huangdi outside Xi'an designed and arranged them to be both fearsome in the afterlife and beautiful to see. The six-five-four-three-two-one-ignition-blast-off giant rockets heading for space from Cape Canaveral and the Baikonur Cosmodrome and Wenchang are designed, I think, to be beautiful and dreadful at the same time in the one thing, the same thing, and out the crowds come to watch, to *feel* the beauty and the threat, out they come, much as the middle class of Boulogne-sur-Mer donned their bonnets, fixed their boutonnière, and called a carriage to take them out to enjoy the military beauty of Napoleon Bonaparte parading his Grand Army in the meadows beyond the town. Out came one-hundred-plus Londoners for a cruise to the Crimea on a paddle steamer called *City of Glasgow* from which they also took day trips with picnic hampers supplied by Fortnum and Mason to the battlefields where there was a war between a British-French-Ottoman-

Piedmont-Sardinia alliance and the Russian Empire, and where the chance to watch men die, British artillerymen hurled high into the air by massive explosions, `their bodies appearing in the distance like birds on the wing,` only added to the beauties of champagne, potted ham, deviled eggs, sunshine, sea, and the steep and lightly wooded shores of the Black Sea at Sevastopol. And how many of us do not swivel our heads and turn our eyes onto a military parade and find it both beautiful and awful?

•

There is yet some Homeric Greek in us, I think, or is it some Nuremberg pumping, some gun, some Prussian corpuscles of the mid-eighteenth-century blood of Herr Professor Doctor Thomas Abbt breast-stroking in our arteries: `When I behold the king surrounded by his brave soldiers, living and dead I am overcome with the thought that it is noble to die fighting for one's fatherland. Now this new beauty that I am reaching for comes more sharply into focus: it delights me; I hasten to take possession of it, tear myself away from anything that could hold me back.`

•

"I love anything in a uniform. Gorgeous," Big Denise says.

•

Some people wonder if Gertrude Stein was a bit hot for soldiers and heroics: `I was a passionate admirer of General Grant.` She had a soft, soft, soft spot for Philippe Pétain, Marshal of France and the Lion of Verdun, a Great War hero, but not dead in battle, and, by 1943, less hero than fool whose collaboration with Adolf Hitler at Montoire in the autumn of 1940 to create the neutral-but-not-neutral French state of Vichy had not turned out well. Still, I can't imagine that Gertrude Stein found Philippe Pétain beautiful or weapons beautiful or war itself beautiful, or any kind of death beautiful (she was, herself, reluctant to go) although maybe she was a bit creamy about doughboys and Ernest Hemingway, goo-goo eyes for those heroes of Italian fascism billeted in the homes of Bilignin. `Well, anyway,` Gertrude Stein might have written at this point, as she does again and again to mark transitions in *Everybody's Autobiography*.

•

Well, anyway: There was that man I fucked who said, "Look at my beautiful cock, would you, and would you like to look at my collection of beautiful military-issue handguns?" I was allowed to touch one, but hands off the other, delicately lit and displayed like a collection of Japanese netsuke or Kutani porcelains in a large vitrine in the living room, where there was also a wide, double-glazed plate-glass window with a distant view of the Jefferson Memorial dome lit like art. There was a Colt Single Action Army first generation 44-40 Win Revolver from about 1880, very valuable, the man I fucked said, but I saw no beauty in it. There was a Ruger MKII Stainless 22LR Pistol, not so valuable, the man I fucked said, yet beauty satined its stainless-steel barrel, I could see *that*, smooth and lethal, the undying beauty of the sword redolent in it, and it terrified me for how this kind of beauty is ever-present. Elaine

Worthy of the Event

Scarry says `Beauty brings copies of itself into being`, beautiful replicates itself, it is viral, which may explain why so many human beings in so many times and so many places find beauty in heroic civilization, in war machines, weapons, war violence and war men, and too few of us, including me, see what Friedrich Nietzsche saw: any beauty that masks the terrible and the hideous is not beautiful at all.

At this point, a.k.a Victor Mature thinks I'm faking it: "That's one of your myriad fabrications," he says. "I don't think Nietzsche said anything like that, did he."

And a.k.a. Victor Mature tells me beauty may be found anywhere, even in ugly, even in this sluggish and uncomfortable train journey through northern Mexico, "But not in men dying for their country," and upon that, a.k.a. Victor Mature disappears to the club car, where there are mezcal and air-conditioning, constant.

✻

What O taught me: 美 is not the only beautiful in Japanese. 美 does beauty duty in utsukushii and many other kinds of beauty, but 美 is not the only beauty. There is flowery uruwashii, which I know mostly from two or three literary and speechifying references to the weather, and has no 美 beauty in it. There is especially kirei, which seems more flexible about beauty than either utsukushii or uruwashii and is as important about beauty as anything 美 does yet has no 美 in it. Kirei uses two characters: one refers to a kind of figured silk twill fabric much admired for its beauty, the other is 麗 which is a more difficult character to write, of course, and is also used for uruwashii beauty, which may imply something more complex about 麗 beautiful than 美 beautiful. I don't know. Anyway, kirei may be used to describe the beauties of art, the view, the human face and body, nature, a K-pop star, Marilyn Monroe, *and* to describe the beauties of clean, neat, tidy, pure, and clear. Some say the distinction between utsukushii and kirei is the distinction between high and low culture, between the ruling class and the rest, between formal and colloquial ideas of beauty in Japan. Some say clean is never an aesthetic condition and so cannot be beautiful. I am unqualified to remark on that, except to note that clean is often a virtue anywhere and beauty is usually a virtue too, especially if you are one of those Neoplatonic types.

I rented beautiful rooms on the upper floor of Mrs. Ikeda's house just a little northwest of the old imperial palace in that not-beautiful district of Kyoto where I liked to live until I discovered the gardens and rice fields, trickling spaces and streams of Iwakura. A sister-in-law in rooms at the back of the house occasionally gave me beautiful painted and lacquered fans disinterred from a paulownia wood chest. Mrs. Ikeda and husband, who seemed habituated to moxibustion, lived below. The moxibustion didn't smell like fun. On the first New Year's Eve, Mrs. Ikeda put out her Mild Seven, mounted the stairs, and presented a quiver of dusters and brooms and cleaning cloths and agents and a vacuum cleaner and a red bucket and a mop with an extendable handle because you are so tall. "Make it all clean," she said, using kirei which meant she might have been saying "Make it all beautiful." I didn't know which meaning kirei had there, but since Mrs. Ikeda had used the imperative form of the verb "to do", I got on alacritous to spraying wiping scrubbing vacuuming sweeping dusting mopping polishing until Mrs. Ikeda doused Mild Seven number fifteen, up the stairs, and scrutiny. "Done!" she said. "You've made it very clean," and a beautiful smile opened on her face. Or is it that Mrs. Ikeda said, "Done. You've made it very beautiful," and a clean smile opened on her face. I don't know.

·

Australian English is wanton with beautiful. Beauty pops up in not the usual beautiful places there, thereby revealing the radical contingency of beauty itself, probably unintentionally: beautiful, Australians might say of a pork sausage, which seems a surprise at first until you realize that beauty does not exist before we say it exists, for beauty relies entirely upon disclosure for its existence. That lucky sausage.

·

It took seventy years for the beauty of Vaslav Nijinsky's *The Rite of Spring* choreography to become beautiful. Critics at the first performances of the ballet in 1913 and 1914 found Nijinsky's steps anything but beautiful and said so, said so vociferously until Léonide Massine was hired to re-choreograph the entire ballet into a form that the critics and the audience could disclose to themselves and the rest of us as beautiful, look, how beautiful the steps. It was not until the 1980s that researchers and Joffrey Ballet recovered the ugly Vaslav Nijinsky choreography from some filing cabinet in a museum or somewhere and staged the ballet, as intended, with Vaslav Nijinsky's steps, which had been so unbeautiful in the before but were now disclosed as extremely beautiful, so beautiful that even were I to think *not*, I lack the spine needed to say, *ugly*.

I don't know who first identified the beauty of J.M.W. Turner's *Venice, from the Porch of Madonna della Salute*. Maybe John Ruskin was the one to say, "How very beautiful this is," while peering at his friend's latest work on the opening day of the 1835 Royal Academy of Arts exhibition in London. Some may not have agreed with John Ruskin upon the beauty of the work at the time. *Venice, from the Porch of Madonna della Salute* seemed unfinished, some said. Some who knew Venice well saw immediately that, in his pursuit of beauty, J.M.W. Turner had made adjustments to Venice in the painting in order to disclose the beauty of Venice the place: he rotated the campanile of St Mark's Cathedral forty-five degrees so that we see it end-on; the view itself is *not* from the porch of Madonna della Salute; he doubled the width of the Grand Canal to make it grander; he painted over the dilapidated, mean, and suffering condition of Venice as it was after the end of the Republic and the occupation by Napoleon. Yet, the painting itself is now *so* beautiful, and in this indisputable beauty, which is also a kind of lie, there might be what Hans-Georg Gadamer calls an `experience of truth` that has nothing to do with either aesthetic theory or the real, but beauty itself. The truth of beautiful Venice in the beautiful painting copies itself onto the truth of Venice the place no matter how flooded, how reeking, how clattering, how stuffed with tourists the city is, no matter how many mammoth cruise ships loom on the waters. "Oh, Venice, so beautiful, it looks just like that Turner painting," Harry says, his muddy eyes shining at it, and I wish *myself* as beautiful as Venice in a Turner painting. Look at *me* like that, go on.

•

Of me, my sister said: bullet head, pig nose, fatty, *hideous*, ugly lump. Mrs. Moller in the red brick house on the corner spoke from slightly on the other side of her usual veils of Rothmans smoke and tincture of opium: "It's no good telling me you want to be beautiful. Little boys don't become beautiful, they become men."

Perhaps pretty, then.

```
Look how pretty I am,
```
Muhammad Ali said when he was still Cassius Clay.
```
My long trim legs and
my beautiful arms and my pretty nose and
mouth. I'm a pretty man, I know I'm pretty
you don't have to tell me I'm pretty.
```
Him and his brothers twisted their bitter mouths upon this improbability. "Pretty," they scoffed and used racial epithets. "And what about the way the bloke *dances* when a man should be fighting. *Pretty*."

Mrs. Moller again: "Pretty is not beautiful. Remember that. If you're going to go on with a hopeless quest, at least think big."

My mother spent hundreds of dollars she might have preferred not to spend putting my sister's nomad teeth on the road to regular beauty. My own incisors and canines were left to break away and wander around my mouth, willy-nilly. My sister told me I looked like an old fence when I smiled. "Don't let the sheep get out." Mr. Shepherd filled *her* decaying back teeth with shining amalgam, but he yanked out mine. My sister whimpered at night because her braces hurt. I made pictures of a beautiful me on the backs of my eyelids, and the next Sunday, I painted my face with oily crayons, green eyelids, magenta lips, and a chocolate brown beauty spot right *there*. I turned a Davy Crockett hat and scraps of lamb's wool and colored paper and my pajama pants into hats and turbans and strapless bodices. I kept my lips closed. I smiled at myself in the mirror, and oh, with those teeth behind painted lips I had become beautiful, more beautiful than *you*, my face had become a beautiful landscape, what a picture I made of my face, and if the beautiful landscape looked like a girl, well then, this is how to be beautiful, I thought, *disappear* into it.

•

That critic of Japanese cinema Donald Richie disappeared from Tokyo to the islands of the Seto Inland Sea in 1968 or 1969 and found `a paradise, an ideal sea garden,` intensely beautiful. The islands are still beautiful now, but it's mostly a silent and unmoving kind of beauty. Back then, the island towns and villages still had plenty of people in them. Ferries shuttled regularly between all the tiny island ports and piers. Back then, the two great leprosaria on Nagashima had thousands of suffering residents. There were farms and orchards and family businesses on the islands then, and local festivals and temples with a priest, and priests with a shrine, and sex workers

Worthy of the Event

here and there, and bars and local gentry and travelling theatrical troupes on the islands (watch *Ukigusa* if you get a chance). Then, those soaring bridges had not yet flung themselves across the beautiful waters, taking the human beauties of the islands with them.

In the book Donald Richie wrote about his travels around the islands of the Seto Inland Sea in 1968 or 1969, he disappears himself into the beautiful landscape and he disappears the landscape into the beautiful people. The beautiful place vanishes into the many beautiful boys and girls Donald Richie fucked or tried to fuck on many of the beautiful islands: Perhaps nowhere on earth is there more beautiful skin than in Japan. Usually hairless, it is not like a mere covering. It is as though the entire body, all the way through, were composed of this soft, smooth lustrousness. I touched her arm. She looked at me, her eyes dark under the darkened sky.

Donald Richie never mentions Ōkunoshima, that beautiful island in the Seto Inland Sea populated with thousands of rabbits and only a short boat ride from the little town of Tadanoumi. Here, the government of imperial Japan manufactured mustard gas, lewisite gas, phosgene gas, hydrogen cyanide gas, tear gas, sternutator gas, and weapons-delivery systems for the gases. The rabbits living on Ōkunoshima now are the great-great-great-great-great-and-many-more-greats-great grandchildren of the rabbits used to test all these poisonous vapors, which the Imperial Japanese Army then released against resistance to Japanese rule in north and northeast China in the 1930s and early 1940s. The endurance of these gas weapons is not as long as the endless life of the beautiful sword, but they do go on. Beautiful Chinese children and sorghum farmers all bronzed and lovely in the Manchurian sun or rosy amid quilts of Jilin snow are even now maimed and killed by chance encounters, and entire villages have been depopulated by accidents with decomposing Japanese poison-gas weapons lying around for more than seventy years in river sands and bamboo groves. Across the Yellow Sea and the Traits of Shimonoseki, the thirteen-, fourteen-, and fifteen-year-old local Japanese girls forced to work in the poison-gas factory on the beautiful island of Ōkunoshima probably had soft, smooth, lustrous, deep skin, all the way through, but years later, that beautiful skin broke out in cankers and ulcers and the girls, who were now women, died of the cruelest kinds of cancer.

※

On the *Aguila Azteca*, three large shots of mezcal in the club car make a Buddhist of a.k.a. Victor Mature. "Some people say impermanence is the ultimate beauty, constant disappearance," he says. Oh, sage. Dawn leaks lavender and candy pink, seams of white fire into the eastern sky. How beautiful. "But impermanent," a.k.a. Victor Mature says, and then, with relish, "And that is so very *difficult*."

Worthy of the Event

This is what *is* difficult: the possibility that the greatest beauty of all beauties may be the beauty of everything fucking off in one way or another. Could it really be that the constant change of all things and all conditions is more beautiful than any *thing* or any *person*, than any gleaming squadron, than the best Japanese skin, than that girl with the charming swagger in her walk, than that art, than a piece of floral jade, that Acropolis, those starry heavens seeming to turn above us, that wet, those shoes, that scimitar, sex on the beach beneath the palm trees, that Angkor Wat, that red amaryllis in the winter window, any beautiful place, that beautiful view of sea and islands? Is everything ending and disappearing more beautiful by far than Anaktoria was beautiful to Sappho, more beautiful than that human relationship which has the power to leave you feeling, as Emily Dickinson puts it, like a crescent of who you were before? a.k.a. Victor Mature says, "Things disappearing is beautiful *and* difficult. You have to say *yes* to it all. Say yes to minunthadios, the most beautiful and the most painful word in any language."

Saying yes: In *The Gay Science*, Friedrich Nietzsche says yes to the beauty of constant change as a part of the formula for greatness in a human being. `I want to learn more and more to see as beautiful what is necessary in things; then I shall be one of those who make things beautiful. Amor fati: let that be my love henceforth! Some day I wish to be only a yes-sayer` to everything including suffering and disaster,

Friedrich Nietzsche means, although it's hard to imagine him talking about "how beautiful" and "amor fati "and saying, "yes, yes, yes" to a tsunami as tall as a twelve-story building, or saying "let this be my love henceforth" while plunging on a summer evening with five hundred others into a Japanese mountain on a Japan Airlines Boeing 747 that has lost its tail.

Saying yes: The Buddha might have been all yes with even the cruelest and most radical kinds of impermanence. He proposes constant change as liberation from all delusions of greatness, and part of the progress toward total kindness: `Dhammapada 227. All created things perish. Those who know and see this become passive in pain; this is the way that leads to purity`. The Buddha is dispassionate about beauty. He is dispassionate about change. No love of fate for him, these things just are. What could be more beautiful than that?

Saying yes: Well, there is the matter of my own mother, who many men found beautiful, and so she *was* beautiful, and who was also as permanent as a woman may ever get. Because of her lifetime commitment to permanence, my mother was steeply inclined to No. She was only Yes, and thus at her most beautiful, when moving in the direction of disappearance, heading for its lip, when leaving (or was it escape), when let's go for a drive. She was never purer, never more beautiful than on those hundreds of long road trips she took more for the sake of going than for Aunt Whoever at the other end. She once drove for five hours through a dark night, winds like fists, rain in slanted sheets, then back again until dawn to rescue me from the side of the highway because my face was too swollen and cut up and my stance too fairy for anybody to see my thumb and give me a lift, and when I apologized for the inconvenience, my mother made no variety of "I'd do anything for my child" response, she just smiled. "Tell me why you look so happy," I said to my mother, and at the wheel of her white Toyota, illuminated by soft light from the dashboard, burnished by her bout of mobility, on the move, she said, "You know. There is hot soup there in the flask."

•

At the end of summer in Oregon, the sea and sky tarnish like neglected silver forks. There are a woman and a giant black poodle on the beach. In the untidy light, the waves suck at themselves, soft ribbons of fog unfurl upon dark necks of rock, and the woman ups her skirts and takes a rake with which she quickly – although it takes two hours – and precisely – although she makes many mistakes and must redo things – etches a great and intricate mandala into the damp sand. She works from center to perimeter. The giant black poodle watches the work. Once or twice, the dog steps wagging into the mandala and out again as though testing the way to heaven. Language passes between the dog and the woman until the dog finally plants its behind on the sand and waits for the woman to finish the last flames in the outermost ring of fire, the burning border across which any seeker must pass before tacking toward the core where exists or does not exist enlightenment itself.

The woman finishes. She lowers her tool to the sand. She lets out a holler. She lets down her skirts and she dances, and the giant black poodle barks and dances too, leaping into the air, twisting, and when their dance is complete, they leave. The swelling tide laps in, tongues the sacred pattern, fresh-made on the sand. What could be more beautiful than this, not so much the beautiful mandala in the sand, not so much the seascape, not the slatternly light, but the woman and the giant poodle *walking away* from their creation without a single backward glance, and most beautiful of all, the disappearance of the mandala itself into the sea, into *absence*.

•

Beautiful Surtsey, fuming and dark, has been saying goodbye since it began. Beautiful Surtsey is constantly moving away from us in the iron sea south of Iceland. Beautiful Surtsey first appeared to the cook aboard a fishing trawler: apparition in the dawn, black pillars of volcanic ash climbing from the Atlantic Ocean, a mountain puts the crown of its head above the water for the first time. Did that cook experience some sublime upon the appearance of an island in the sea or was it fear at the arrival? Beautiful Surtsey, within a fortnight forming a brittle island of scoria rock, which is like heavy pumice, and hardened lava, rising one hundred and fifty-five meters above the sea. Within two years of Surtsey's beautiful birth, diatoms appeared in the littoral and soon the seaweed, Ulothrix, green and filamented, and then, quickly, colonies of vascular plants upon the new land: sea rocket, which is a mustard and has pretty but not beautiful white and purple flowers in the summer; sea sandwort, an edible purslane and vividly green; sea lyme grass, used by Inuit, Cupiit, and Yup'ik peoples for weaving;

three types of willow; ferns and horsetails; mosses; lichens. Spiders appeared. Great black-back and herring gulls arrived and nested, formed colonies, and shat all over the place, opening Surtsey to permanent settlers: earthworms, beetles, snails, butterflies, and fleas. Common seals haul out for winter on Surtsey now, and in autumn, gray seals breed on the northern spit. Yet, beautiful Surtsey dies as it lives, and that is why beautiful Surtsey is beautiful. Each year Surtsey loses some of itself, the island walks away on wind and high surf, and at some time in the future, Surtsey will be gone, or it will be just a dusty bone of itself, like you and I one day, barely a memory there, the land will be sea again and the sea will be land again. This is not a wheel; it is the exquisitely beautiful walking of mountains.

•

Giorgione's *La Vecchia* may never disappear from us now. Even were the waters of the Laguna di Venezia to rise up and suck the entire Gallerie dell'Accademia down to the silty bottom and *La Vecchia* with it; even were the airplane carrying La Vecchia for a visit to the Cincinnati Art Museum to plummet from the heavens in flames, the *aura* of *La Vecchia* would endure, indelible, permanent, constantly circulated by all the copies *La Vecchia*'s beauty has made of itself in prints, museum catalogues, jpegs, pngs, tiffs, minds, ineradicable until human beings finally off themselves entirely, and even then there will be a tabby cat or a mollusk that appreciates art. Is there not, though, something at odds in the ineradicable permanency of *La Vecchia* as beauty itself and the mission of the painting, which is to disclose and represent, realistically, the many lineaments of old age as beauty? The woman is luminous, worn down to exquisite erosions. Her face is a waterfall of experience. In her right hand, a small paper notice inscribed with "Col tempo": So it happens with Time. Which is most beautiful here? The beautiful repute of *La Vecchia*, Giorgione's painting itself, or the unstoppable changes and disappearances it describes, our universal path unto death?

·

Some Buddhist texts recommend the practitioner `first go to a mound to observe the stages of a decaying corpse, such as the stage of turning bluish black; for a deeper contemplation, step back and sit at a place and contemplate the image again`. Other instructive stages are fresh corpse, bloated corpse, corpse leaking stale blood and fluids, corpse now bluish black, desiccated corpse, corpse eaten by animals, skeleton, scattered bones, and dust. All states of decomposition disclose the beauty of endings and uncontrollable change. All teach us to *see* the beauty of it.

On the dock at Koh Mak, where twelve people wait under the probing sun for the fast boat to Trat, this monk shares his bright golden parasol with me. I give him a wad of baht, which must be more than the worth of the shade cast by the bright golden parasol because this monk delivers a homily: "Make an autopsy on yourself. Cut yourself open. Look at your innards. Touch your *personal filaments*. Put your fingers on your liver. There. Then you will know how everything does not last, and you will love what you know. You will see the beauty of it." I put my hands together and I bow, and the fast boat for Trat comes in. The sea is choppy.

Worthy of the Event

The spray turns to salt in my hair and when I look back, the bright golden parasol has gone from the picture.

•

Seven pictures of Fairy, who is somewhere else being beautiful now, who knows where. I could find it but I would rather see Fairy's `lovely walk`, that slightly arrogant `saunter and the radiant sparkle of her face` in a picture or in a memory than in some encounter with Fairy again in life where I might face again the yearning for unchanging:

Picture #1: Fairy in plaid pajamas grinning and pink and drinking me in because I have used brown liquid eyeliner to paint the moustache of a cavalier on her top lip which somehow makes her even more beautiful than she is.

Picture #2: Fairy in Kassel misses me in Istanbul already. She sends me this selfie still wearing her this-is-serious-business deep blue suit. The lighting in her room at the Novostar Hotel casts upon Fairy in a way that turns her skin to ivory and her lips morello cherry red and enigmatic, but I know what Fairy wants: she wants to make me here and there present forever.

Picture #3: Fairy on the parquet floor of that almost empty apartment overlooking the Bosporus. She looks at me or at the camera as though what she sees might beatify, not beautify, her.

Picture #4: Fairy stands in the shallow end of the horizon pool with a view of the Straits of Malacca behind her. I aim the camera. Warm rain jewels the lens and Fairy beckons, saying to me, "Come in, come in, darling, and swim between my legs."

Picture #5: It's at a diner down the street from Lechmere Station on the Green T Line and though Fairy's profile is beautiful, there is no not seeing the No in the angle of head.

Picture #6: At that glassy bookshop in Erfurt and Fairy is as rigid as bone. She looks at me but not at me. I can no longer see into her aquarium eyes.

The seventh picture I have of Fairy is what Maria Stepanova might call a memory of a memory. In what I remember of what I remember, we fuck in the before-dawn shadows of the great city. So close to it, Fairy looks like beauty, she looks at me, she looks like she might stay, she is cinematic. Fairy's swollen lips, her blooming cheeks, her breasts are like some fat `Technicolor chrysanthemums`, but her cries and the heaving remind me of Sigourney Weaver in *Alien Resurrection*, which is a cheap image, I know. I can't help it, I can't help wondering if something terrifyingly new may burst from Fairy's chest, or from anywhere on me, or from the great city outside where the müezzin down the street calls fajr, `Prayer is better than sleep. Prayer is better than sleep`, but looking at Fairy is better than sleep, then, now, forever, to see the beauty that cannot be kept, no matter how much I want it.

"If they knew," Fairy says.

"It is Istanbul not Riyadh," say I.

※

Some people find a kind of beauty in making other kinds of beauty die; you should kill it before it kills you. In 1950 and one of those hot, wet nights you get in Kyoto in July, a novice monk by the name of Hayashi Yoken set fire to the gilded fourteenth-century pavilion known as Kinkakuji, part of the Rokuonji Zen complex. Kinkajuji was renowned for its great beauty then; it is a UNESCO World Heritage Site now and thought to be one of the most beautiful buildings in the world. You have to like gold. In the novel *Kinkakuji*, Mishima Yukio, who was all for heroic civilization and found beauty in military matters, in war, war machinery, and valiant death in battle, depicts the young Buddhist arsonist as so ugly and tormented by his ugliness that he cannot bear beauty. He cannot bear beautiful Kinkakuji, and after weeks of planning and a final inventory of all the golden pavilion's beauties, he `crouched down by the straw and this time struck two matches together` and whoosh, the great beauty was gone.

•

A team of Czech and Azerbaijani researchers found that the beauty of a snake correlates to fear of a snake. The more beautiful the snake, the more dangerous, some people feel: run from the beautiful, glistening serpent or kill kill kill before the beauty of the beautiful snake kills you. Beauty terrifies us, Rainer Maria Rilke says: `For beauty is nothing but the beginning of terror, which we still are just able to endure, and we are so awed because it serenely disdains to annihilate us`. Beauty suggests a higher form of reality to Rilke, so high, it may be unreal, sidereal even, alien, or the power of angels, gods and celestials, oh, bow down to the floor or die, you. That radical Whig, Edmund Burke, thought beauty a delightful horror, and when I read what Burke has to say about beauty, I wonder if there may be a lost Sappho poem lost somewhere, completely disappeared but waiting for the light; a poem considering the horrifying potential of Anakatoria's sublime beauty, and Sappho wondering whether erotic beauties might be just as awful as the beauty of a host of cavalry, a fleet of ships, and heroic death in battle.

・

As you know, to put the eyes on beauty is to put the eyes on death, Luchino Visconti says in some interview about his 1971 movie, *Death in Venice*.

・

Some say trans anything is beautiful and are talking about themselves. Some say trans anything is beautiful and are talking politics, for there is some idea that beauty might be a precursor of liberation. Some say trans anything is beautiful and chase it. Some people have mixed feelings about trans beauty. Some people want it, and wanting it makes them want to burn it, hit it, run away from it, jeer at it, blame it, prohibit it; they are frightened to death by the beauty they find in or on trans women although the death is usually the trans woman's death, not some people's.

We called Chook Robyn Chook Robyn because we were all in Sydney and chook is Australian slang for chicken, and Chook Robyn had the head of a chicken, you know, almost no chin, really, a set of wattles, a tiny mouth inclined to petulance and squawks, a low, sloped forehead usually hidden beneath Clairol Cleopatra Blue Black bangs, and in the middle of it all, a nose as sharp as the beak of any Rhode Island Red. Chook Robin also had the kind of Marilyn-Monroe-Beyonce-Kim-Novak-Scarlett-Johansson body estrogen sometimes gives.

Men who thought KFC when they saw Chook Robyn's head had the pleasure of involuntary ejaculations at the sight of her beautiful body, which Chook handled like a hula dancer, so light, graceful, so rich in meaning. The men had to have it, and Chook Robyn gave it, why not? But at some point, after the men got what they wanted more than three or four times, the men took to punching, beating, sneering, yelling, kicking, backhanding, and even, on three occasions, knifing Chook Robyn.

Little Carol thought the problem was the contradiction of Rhode Island Red face and head upon Marilyn-Monroe-Beyoncé-Kim-Novak-Scarlett-Johansson body.

Big Denise said, "Pull the other leg. It sings the national anthem. You can put a bag over the head, but you can't put a bag over the dick, can you? That's the problem."

Well, there *were* ways and means with dicks, but Big Denise had so many rules and rigid niceties about each and every one of her own sexual encounters, she knew nothing of those ways with dicks. And, in a way, Big Denise was right: the men hated themselves for wanting *all* of Chook Robyn's beautiful body, penis included. Oh, their stories about it went, I didn't really want it, She made me feel it. I was forced into desire. That beautiful Marilyn-Monroe-Beyoncé-Kim-Novak-Scarlett-Johansson body with penis attacked me and I fought back. I was in fear of my life.

•

"You are one of those men who thinks trans is beautiful and chases it and then gets himself caught and spends the rest of the affair trying to show he's not caught at all. You are unworthy of the event. That is you; that is my opinion," Norma Mapagu said to a.k.a. Victor Mature after a bit too much chardonnay and weed.

a.k.a. Victor Mature gave Norma Mapagu a blast from violent eyes.

"Hurrah," Norma Mapagu said.

•

I sometimes think about Anaktoria's facial angle and whether it was or was not the sublime ideal of one hundred degrees devised as the ultimate measure of human beauty by the Greek sculptors and painters of Sappho's time Was Anaktoria's facial angle so gorgeously steep no sharp ocean-going prow nor acutely angled spear or sword could rival Anaktoria for Sappho's affections?

Nineteenth-century ethnologists estimated the average facial angle of the Indigenous peoples of what is now Australia to be eighty-five degrees, much steeper than the twenty-degree facial angle of a dog but impossible to be a beautiful, intelligent human being like that, they said at the same time as they scritched the twenty-degree angled faces of their setters and labs and collies and whippets and beagles and sausage dogs (not pekes or pugs) and said, oh smart dog, oh beautiful dog.

No matter the acuity or not of any facial angle, Mary Wollstonecraft had ideas about the beauty of Indigenous women. Indigenous women, she thought, were beautifully untrammeled. But the beauty Mary Wollstonecraft saw in Indigenous women had nothing to do with Indigenous women and everything to do with transformation of white women's lives in late-eighteenth-century England and Europe. For Mary Wollstonecraft, Indigenous women were beautiful for the lesson they taught about the female face and body liberated from the oppressions of corsets, voluminous and modest dress, primping, tweezing, perfuming, dainty, deportment, comportment, and encasements.

As a child on unceded Wiradjuri land, I almost never saw a Wiradjuri person or any of the other First Nations people who lived in and around the town. Nobody mentioned the angle of Wiradjuri faces, but what I was taught was that Aboriginal men and women were indisputably ugly, that even Lois Briggs, who was a model and Miss Melbourne in 1961, was only as beautiful as she possibly was because of all that white blood and remember that you can't trust the pretty, pale ones because *they* throw back unpredictably and her baby could be as ugly and as black as the rest of them, and anyway, they're all disappearing, eventually.

※

a.k.a. Victor Mature disappears from the *Aguila Azteca*. The guard advises tranquility please and "Why not a little disembarkation at San Luis Potosí, perfectly understandable, do you know the old city has a number of important and very beautiful Baroque buildings in the Mexican style and of course graceful parks, and, of course also, enchiladas potosí."

The guard has the club-car waiter bring mezcal to the cama matrimoinial. I add two blue diazepam. Tranquility makes its appearance, and I go on to Mexico City a bit *sprawled*, even akimbo, in that little compartment suddenly large. a.k.a. Victor Mature reappears five days later at the Hotel Versailles, which has a beautiful cocktail lounge done out with divans and gauze draped like the veils of Salome and lit by tender crayon-colored spotlights and will itself disappear in the 1985 earthquake.

I ask why.

a.k.a. Victor Mature gives me flamethrower eyes about why so we go down to the beautiful cocktail bar and lie on divans and finger the beautiful gossamer drapes in the pink and primrose lights and listen to jazz and drink mezcal, and later, a.k.a. Victor Mature vomits torrents in the shower, once, twice, six times between midnight and four, so much of him going down the drain. He vomits so hard and so often I think his bronchial tubes might fly out of his mouth, his lungs, his stomach, his colon, his asshole, even, spewed onto the pink tiles and swirling down the drain into the lake still there somewhere below the city. I wonder if a.k.a. Victor Mature is disappearing again. Just go, if you want to go.

a.k.a. Victor Mature goes from a hotel in Vero Beach. He disappears from a Delta Airlines Lockheed Tristar about to close its doors at Atlanta for the flight to La Guardia. He disappears into the hot night in Colombo and gone for weeks. a.k.a. Victor Mature disappears from dinner parties and backyard barbeques, from the middle of Act 2 of *King Lear,* from a box at the Booth Theater as soon as David Bowie makes his entrance in *The Elephant Man*, from the opening credits at the world premiere of the first *Mad Max* movie. a.k.a. Victor Mature almost disappears permanently one pouring morning when he drives my red Alfa Romeo GTV high speed into the back of a parked truck. "What the fuck were you doing?" I say.

From his hospital bed a.k.a. Victor Mature says, "I saw a beautiful black star with your father on it."

We call this event The Accident. We never say Suicide Attempt.

a.ka. Victor Mature disappears to Caracas. He disappears into the sky in a Nimbus 2 sail-plane, up up up into the cumulus towers and gone, he goes, and when he has not returned to the field eight hours later, there is talk of calling the police but then, oh, a.k.a. Victor Mature drops yonder, blazing like a shard of fire in the lowering sun. "Here I am," he says.

Oh, how a.k.a. Victor Mature disappears. He is a disappearing act. He disappears from home a dozen times in nine years. He wants me to see how fast he goes. He tells me I am beautiful, and I am. He wants me to recognize the beauty of things disappearing, he wants me to do the beautiful thing and let him go, and I do, I do, I do. I am diligent. I do see the great, implausible beauty of impermanence. I see it, I see it until I see too much to see it again. I see it until I see myself disappearing. On pink Post-It notes, I write Mahalo and aloha nui loa and any other Hawaiian word that may signify both departure *and* to where I am disappearing, for gone does not necessarily mean over, does it? On a yellow Post-It note in the large size, I write, How beautiful it is to disappear. And I go.

a.k.a. Victor Mature watches me going. He drives me to the airport and seems impassive as I vanish, but Norma Mapagu tells me later that before I even reached cruising altitude on Air New Zealand, a.k.a. Victor Mature wept and gnashed his not-so-beautiful teeth and did not feed the cat, and it went on for weeks, his grief over disappearance about which he had always insisted: beautiful.

Recently, I heard, also from Norma Mapagu, that a.k.a. Victor Mature is living now in an apartment in the Ermita district of Manila, although I suspect Norma Mapagu might be hiding something from me about that. She does. I am not sure a.k.a. Victor Mature has gone so far. I've caught glimpses of him on Platform Ten at the station. I saw those wide lips coming the other way down the mountain road in a tiny green Lotus Elan, its fiberglass monocoque unruffled as though just off the showroom floor. It must have been a.k.a. Victor Mature looking disappointed in the dark at that Matsui Yayoi installation. It must be a.k.a. Victor Mature who sends me that email on my birthday, no good wishes in it, just a scan of a page from some book or magazine upon which, a poem by Voltaire Q. Oyzon in a language I do not know and an English translation.

I take the language I don't know to be Tagalog. Norma Mapagu knows better. "What would *you* know about it," she says. "This is Waráy. The language of Leyte and Samar, Eastern Visayas. It is a bit disappearing these days."

In her sweet and nearly beautiful voice, Norma Mapagu reads the poem to me twice, first the Waráy and then the English, and when she reads, there are no dot dot dots in it and nothing disappears from it:

Worthy of the Event

<u>'Buklara an Imo mga Palad'</u>[1]

para han matugdon
nga ogis nga sarapati
nga mapakadto,
mapakanhi

sugad han pagpatugdon
han puno han lubi
ha pagal nga tamsi
ha iya idinudupa nga mga palwa.

Abata an iya kagaan,
an iya kabug-at.
Pamatia an iya ighuhuni,
an iya ig-aaraba.
Kulawi an iya kaanyag,
ngan ha takna
nga iya na bubuklaron
an iya nakapahuway na
nga mga pako,
alsaha an imo butkon,
ig-undong hiya
nga't ha langit,

ngan hinumdomi
paglimot.

---

[1] It is a privilege to be able to share "Buklara an Imo mga Palad" here in the form intended and requested by the poet, Voltaire Q. Oyzon (Leyte Normal University): Waráy on the left and his English translation on the right. Thanks to Efmer E. Agustin (University of the Philippines Tacloban) for introducing me to Prof. Oyzon.

Vivian Blaxell

<u>'Open Your Hands'</u>

to catch
the white dove
in its coming
and going

the way the palm tree
receives the tired bird
seeking refuge
in its wide-flung fronds.

Feel its lightness,
its weight.
Hear what it has to sing,
what it is pleading for.
Enjoy its loveliness,
and when the time comes
for it to stretch
its wings that have rested,
lift up your arms
and toss it
to the skies,

and remember
to forget.

I find the email address of Voltaire Oyzon and I write requesting permission to use his poem here at the end of beauty and its disappearances, and he replies:

Worthy of the Event

Of course! What is the purpose of beauty if it's not shared?

V: indifferent to prayer

They are digging dead children out of the mud up in Ōtsuchi, Minamisōma, Ishinomaki. O shows up in the lobby of the hotel in Okayama. The hotelier is also a milliner. She uses the hotel lobby to sell her hats. O is so short she vanishes beneath any hat. Even so, she tries an indigo and beige boater, a beret rakish in crimson raffia, a white sun bonnet upon which, the slogan MilkRun for some reason. Before O tries each hat, she waves a cellphone-sized radiation detector over it. "Don't cry about that Fairy woman," she says. "You are now too old for such feelings. There is much more to face up to than broken hearts."

O gives up on the hats and roams the not-very-big-lobby with her radiation detector held out in front of her face like some kind of extra nose. Click. Click. Later, she turns the radiation detector onto the Family Mart where we buy a packet of Seven Stars, click click click. Out it comes for signs of iodine-131 (half-life 8.02 days), click, cesium-137 (half-life 30 years), click, cesium-134 (half-life 2.06 years), click, every hundred meters or so of our stroll in the innocent sunshine through the avenues and emerald swathes of Kōraku-en. She interrogates the green peaks of our matcha sofutokuriimu cones for death, disease, gruesome deformity or all three and pronounces them clean enough. "But you can't trust milk products now. Cows absorb radioisotopes like sponges take up water," O says, but when I ask O how she *feels*, she says the disaster didn't happen to her, and in a way O is right. It is the twenty thousand people up in Fukushima, Ōtsuchi, Minamisōma, Ishinomaki, Sendai who are dead; it's their families and communities wounded and homeless and terrified of the future; it's the animals washed out to sea or abandoned to their own devices who got it. Yet, in a way, O is wrong: the 2011 earthquake, tidal wave, and meltdown of Tokyo Electric Company's nuclear reactors at Nahara in Fukushima happened to her, happened to all of us, only with differing effects and consequences.

※

Miss Sybil Fontaine, whom we called Old Sybil only when there was one hundred percent no chance of Miss Sybil Fontaine hearing us call her Old Sybil, was in her late-forties then and famous among us for truculence with fists, if required, and if not required, dedication to the fashion principles of a society matron in the eastern suburbs of Sydney in 1972, high-end blow jobs, and premonitions. Miss Sybil Fontaine never appeared anywhere at any time without a suit that could have been Chanel, but was not; she never appeared in winter unwarmed by an overcoat that might have been Aquascutum but was not. As far as we knew, Miss Sybil Fontaine never left the house without a hat that could have been a hat from Manhattan milliners but was not. She never showed up without her blunt but beautifully kept hands clad in black or charcoal kid gloves in winter and white cotton gloves in summer and she was never there without her also blunt feet shod in *real* Ferragamo pumps, and Miss Sybil Fontaine never went anywhere without perfect Dior Trans-Siberian-Express-red lips (real) in a full upper bow, also real. She had beautiful lips and a Delphic approach to the future.

Miss Sybil Fontaine charged a lot for her services. We wondered if Miss Sybil Fontaine gave those expensive blow jobs with her Manhattan-but-not-Manhattan hat in place and her not-quite-Chanel suit crisp and prim around her knees, which might be why her blow jobs commanded such high fees, we said, who knows, *kink*. Miss Sybil Fontaine's Delphic abilities seemed self-fulfilling to me, but terrifying, nonetheless. She once said to me, "Get the fuck off this corner. It's mine, it's always been mine. It's mine until I say it's not mine. Get off now or I'll flatten you," and when I fled up the nighttime hill in my pink and red paisley pants and white halter top, Miss Sybil Fontaine shouted to my back, "You'll be fine. You've got survivor oozing out of your pores."

News went around that the Royal Prince Alfred Hospital was starting a sex change program. Some of the girls who wanted vaginas got all excited. Most of the rest anticipated liberation, maybe, from the moody authority of Pharmacist-Blake-near-the-fountain for under-the-counter diethyl-stilbestrol tablets, which he sometimes withheld just because and always charged five times what the stilboestrol would cost if you had a prescription, fat chance. Even Trixie Lamont was said to have made an appointment to be assessed for the two-year assessment preceding the final assessment for neovagina.

Not true.

Miss Sybil Fontaine saw only **big trouble** in it. Hat and suit and Italian pumps and gloves and Dior Trans-Siberian-Express perfect, Miss Sybil Fontaine came into that coffee shop near the fire station at the usual time of nine-thirty-five pm and cleared girls off her usual table with her usual just one look. She seated herself as usual, and, as ever, she tugged at each fingertip of each charcoal kid glove, arching her hands back like a Balinese dancer until the gloves came off. As usual, Miss Sybil Fontaine drank an extra-hot cappuccino, nibbled at a slice of raisin toast, and smoked two of those gold foil tipped Sobranie Black Russian cigarettes she was never ever without.

Now: the iron rule was that girls never sat at Miss Sybil Fontaine's table when Miss Sybil Fontaine was seated at it. The law was that girls never spoke to Miss Sybil Fontaine at the coffee shop unless previously addressed by Miss Sybil Fontaine, but Big Denise was high on something that night, diet pills, trying to be smaller, red pills, a whole box of NoDoz, I don't know, and impromptu, she asked Miss Sybil Fontaine if Miss Sybil Fontaine would be applying to the new sex change program. The impertinence of speaking before spoken-to struck the whole coffee shop dumb, silent, except for Dusty doing "Son of a Preacher Man" on the jukebox and Mr. Doddy fluffing cappuccino foam at the Gaggia. Miss Sybil Fontaine lit up a third gold-tipped

Black Russian and smoked it very thoughtful right down to the gold foil tip. Unspeaking, unmoving, she was, smoking, except for the arc of her right hand with Black Russian to Dior Trans-Siberian-Express lips and back to table. Three and a half minutes and agonizing it took, the wait for what was certain to come, some curse, some prediction, a scythe of mockery, string of oaths, depending on what, we knew not, so we tried not breathing. Eventually, Miss Sybil Fontaine said, "What I see here is you fucking queens turning into lab rats, jumping through square people's hoops to get a box put in, and no good can come from that. Disaster. Not all disasters are earthquakes, or plane crashes, or going broke, getting the wrong end of Hilda Handcuffs. Some disasters look good until they hit you and then the consequences. You will be vulnerable."

Big Denise's whatever-pills had made her so buzzed she'd forgotten about consequences and how to stop and she said, "Anything's better than being a freak, don't you think, Miss Sybil Fontaine?" at which Miss Sybil Fontaine pursed her Trans-Siberian-Express lips from beautiful to nasty for thirty seconds. More breath-holding on our part, there will be blood. Then she said, "Do you know that wild rats die if they are handled. It's not like those doctors have *our* best interests uppermost in their minds. I see the end of us girls. I do. They will turn us into Hottentot Venuses. The bearded woman at the circus will have it better than us. We will not survive as ourselves."

Had I known the word, "hyperbole", then, I might have used it at that moment, but I just thought, oh, crazy Old Sybil, I mean what could possibly be disastrous about

Worthy of the Event

becoming more woman unless, you know, you bled out or something. But, less than two years later, there came the news that Barbra had taken sixty-nine too many Seconal caps the day after Dr. Ron Barr had told her the neovagina-or-not-final-assessment-committee had ruled not, no, never, no appeal on Barbra's neovagina because that test with pornographic pictures and electrodes attached to Barbra's dick showed Barbra liked girls too much for any sort of vagina at all. Plus, Barbra's jaw, we supposed, and facial feminization surgery still below the yonder horizon.

•

```
You manipulate people in an unconscious
fashion as a part of an overall type of manip-
ulativeness that we have come to recognize
as part and parcel of the personalities of
many individuals with gender disorders.
Let me say candidly that at this point in
time you are not deemed, for your own best
interests, a good candidate for immediate
sex conversion, and we cannot give you a
definite date in the future other than to
say you are on a hold status.
```

•

To be honest, Barbra had broken into my room, lifted my stereo player, and hocked it at Gorman's Pawn and Loan, and I wanted, without much hope, a way to blast *Electric Ladyland* and Aretha Franklin and John Coltrane and the Moody Blues and Quicksilver Messenger Service, *Surrealistic Pillow* and Gustav Holst at myself and the neighbors again, so the mean part of me thought crematorium and black star for Barbra might be fair, but the other part of me wondered if Miss Sybil Fontaine been right about the consequences of the cisgender-heterosexual-maybe-doctor-with-a-research-agenda and transsexual girl patient relationship. I shuffled, cut, and shuffled The Tarot and got The Tower. Oh, God. How was I to be to be worthy of *that*?

✳

Harry was the kind of man who expected disaster to come for him all day every day waking sleeping eating. He was so on tenterhooks for a car accident that he could barely drive, I mean, he drove, but at any intersection without lights, Harry could not make a decision to turn, when to turn, now, later, too late, when, and his head swiveled left to right so many times I wanted to throw up or slap him, and once I said at an intersection near the Pentagon, "Oh, for fuck's sake, just drive into that UPS eighteen-wheeler and put us all out of your uncertainty."

"You are sometimes very mean. I'm only trying to be safe," Harry said and stamped on the gas.

Who knows how Harry feels these days, with Kīlauea leaking lava into his back garden and the world simultaneously burning and drowning and choking, and novel viruses running things. Stalked by risk he feels, perhaps, like native Hawaiians must have felt stalked by smallpox and measles after Europeans arrived in the islands, although native Hawaiians did not feel stalked by lava which was then and is now a godly substance.

Worthy of the Event

✶

L's second sister-in-law even looks like a cow, she really does, in a good way; she is one of those beautiful cows with huge, soft eyes, satiny and fringed with great lashes, and her nostrils are cavernous and sueded like pussy willow and always looking at you, and she has large breasts which seem to want you to consider them for a position, and L does not like her sister-in-law and calls her cow, not in a good way, although now the sister-in-law has had major surgery in another city, and even though L does not like the sister-in-law, L cares, and L is a *nurse*, and nurses *do* have some kind of public reputation to uphold, so dutiful Nurse L takes the early flight up, arrives on time, and lines up at the cab rank outside the terminal, waits five minutes, gets into the back seat of a silver cab, buckles in. The sea glitters. Hosts of white cockatoos mob the trees and clamorous. The traffic into town is heavy but moving fast. Close to the hospital where the sister-in-law is smiling and happy (oh, those pain meds make me feel blissful like successful breast-feeding, press the button again, *please*) the highway dips beneath the ground without slowing and suddenly, unexpectedly it seems, though of course *not* unexpected from Paul Virilio's standpoint, L's cab veers, swerves, mounts the tunnel wall, ricochets off into the air and lands on its side, broken and slewed across two lanes. L is still in her belt but bleeding beneath her skin where the belt crosses her breasts and belly, and one of her legs is shattered. She ends up in a bed eight floors below the bed of her sister-in-law. L ends up ruined by this millions-of-times-every-day disaster *invented* by technology: the internal-combustion engine, steel-reinforced concrete, the tunnel, the science of traffic management, and most of all, the invention of speeding objects and *speed* itself. L feels star-crossed. "It's a bitch being Sagittarius with all that Scorpio in me," she says and angry and wanting God or the cosmos or something ineffable to blame, but L's disaster can't just be something untoward and fateful, written in the stars. L's disaster was almost certain at some point, immanent to the automobile itself.

✷

A great white shark took a young man at Little Bay, came up on him as he swam in the summery waters and bit him hugely, severed his torso, tore his body into two pieces, one of which vanished out to sea. A police hunt for the missing half and for the specific great white shark began almost immediately. Drum lines with savage baited hooks unfurled in the beautiful waters, and nobody says how many sharks died on it, but we do know a man died in two separate bleeding pieces. For whom was the disaster greatest, the man or the sharks of the Tasman Sea? What did the man feel in the time of the disaster itself as the great serrated army of teeth went in and tore him into two. Did he look down and think in an objective way, "my God, my bottom has gone, I was one, now I am two"? What did those sharks dying on the drum line feel in the moment of their final disaster?

Worthy of the Event

✺

```
Mariko, Tsuyoshi, Chiyoko, be good to each
other and work hard. Help your mother.
It's sad, but I'm sure I won't make it.
I don't know the cause. It's been five
minutes now. I don't want to take any more
planes. Please kami-sama help me. To think
that our dinner last night was the last
time. There was some sort of explosion in
the cabin. There was smoke and we started
to descend. Where are we going, what will
happen? Tsuyoshi, I'm counting on you.
Darling, it's too bad that this has hap-
pened. Goodbye. Please take good care of
the children. It's 6:30 now. The plane is
turning around and descending rapidly. I
am grateful for the truly happy life I
have enjoyed until now.[2]
```

•

There is a photograph taken through a window of Japan Airlines Flight 123 as it climbs out of Haneda shortly after six in the early evening light of August 12, 1985, and in that photograph, you can see the bronzed cast Tokyo Bay and the skies toward Fujisan take on in late summer at the end of another hot and humid day. There is high stratus. It is O-bon, the season when dead relatives return to this world for a visit. There are five

[2] Kawaguchi Hirotsugu, JL123, August 12, 1985

hundred and nine people going to their hometowns to visit family and the ancestors or heading home to Osaka, to Nara or Kyoto even Kobe after an O-bon season getaway in Tokyo. The five hundred and nine include a famous singer and actor and the senior executive of a famous curry company, many children. There is a crew of fifteen. At twenty-four thousand feet and about ten minutes after takeoff, many of the five hundred and nine passengers and fifteen crew hear a **pān** sound, or it might be more than one sound, **dodōdodon** or **dodōn**, it is an explosion or explosions, and although none of the five hundred and nine passengers and fifteen crew know it, the great bulk-head at the far rear of the Boeing 747 has failed, burst open and back and taken much of the tail fin and vertical stabilizer and all the hydraulic control systems with it. There is immediately no chance of anything other than a great accident, which happens about half an hour later after a terrifying, looping ride, something horrible called a Dutch roll over and over again, sickening, and deathly yawing, and very little oxygen, a futile and uncontrolled circling until the aircraft dives and plunges upside down into a ridge, bodies and body pieces strewn in the beautiful mountains of Gunma where bird catchers once captured hawks to be sent to Edo for training as hunters for the shogun of the day for whom hawking was an expected pastime even if he didn't particularly care for it. Five hundred and twenty died. Four survived. Unpredictable mechanical failure caused by an unpredictable mistake in a previous repair of the rear bulkhead, investigators concluded, although To get what is heavier than

```
air to take off in the form of an aeroplane
or dirigible is to invent the crash, the
air disaster.
```

※

On the morning of All Saints Day 1755, thousands of the faithful packed Lisbon's forty churches offering their myriad devotions until, in the midst of communion or some hosanna, Lisbon itself began to groan and shake, ten thousand fissures as wide as a living room opened in Baixa, and the naves and apses, the flying buttresses and domes, and the stained glass windows telling the Bethlehem story and all the rest in thirty of the forty Lisbon churches sundered and fell upon the worshippers and the altar boys and the priests, and before the consecrated rubble had quite stilled, a tidal wave rushed up the Tagus River, and fires broke out so intense they sucked the air out of the lungs of people far from the blaze. Between thirty and sixty thousand people died.

Debate, so widespread and sophisticated it included Immanuel Kant and Voltaire, began upon the causes and meanings of the earthquake, tidal wave, and inferno: Was the disaster a moral subject or a natural phenomenon? The question itself and the great public discussion of it were quite new. Only seventy-five years previous, the earthquake that had turned Malaga to rubble had been explained as God's punishment for the sins of the people of the city, and no voice raised in disagreement, God did it, atone, repent.

The Lisbon priests tried the same story after the earthquake and the rest but there was by then a kind of Baruch Spinoza effect upon the matter of God, and Enlightened men like the man who would become the Marquês de Pombal, and even the king of Portugal himself, were not having it. God certainly created the planet and everything in it, but he did not make the planet do things like earthquake to punish decent Portuguese for their improper fornications, their petty larcenies, or even for the greater sins of the state: conquest, slavery, global empire, *Brazil*. Even when the science was wrong, a scientific view of the causes of earthquakes prevailed. The modern science of earthquakes began here.

The Marquês de Pombal had a survey drawn up and administered to priests, convents and monasteries, and to officials in Lisbon, in Lisbon's surrounds, and in the Algarve: How long did the earthquake last. How many shocks were felt. What kind of damage was caused. Did animals behave strangely. What happened in wells and water holes. Responses were collected, collated, quantified, applied to planning, used for prediction, and it was at this point that modern technology not only began to analyze, prepare for, and predict both accidents and disasters both natural and unnatural, but in the analysis, preparation, and prediction of disaster, technologies of inquiry and technologies of things, came to invent the accident and the disaster themselves. `The riddle of technology is also the riddle of the accident,` **Paul Virilio thinks.** `Every technology produces, provokes, programmes a specific accident.`

Worthy of the Event

```
For example: when they invented the rail-
road, what did they invent? An object that
allowed you to go fast, which allowed you
to progress - a vision à la Jules Verne,
positivism, evolutionism. But at the same
time, they invented the railway disaster.
```

※

I once saw sake cups totter and fall to the floor, two blue roof tiles tiles spin out and come back to the house like boomerangs. I saw the ugly little marmalade cat with the crooked tail jamming herself beneath the bed. I saw my framed and very valuable print of the market in Japanese-occupied Mukden, 1933, fall from the wall and the glass shatter. I saw how the horizon toward Hieizan seemed to heave its spine into the wintery morning light, then slump, so quick, it was. I saw the pulse of blood in my wrist. On NHK, I saw more than six thousand dead and forty-five thousand homeless, but not me, not Harry. I was not close enough to the epicenter. It was not my time for the black star. I did not lose my home, an eye, a mother, a husband, a child, and the city did not come down upon me and burn.

Norma Mapagu says there's a difference between natural and unnatural disasters. "You should know that," she says. "You should know that earthquakes are a natural disaster and do not require technology of any kind to invent them."

I am not one to argue with Norma Mapagu. Who is?

Also, the idea that some disasters are natural and others unnatural is one point of view.

Not mine.

A natural earthquake is one that occurs without affecting human life, human structures, and so on. The natural earthquake becomes unnatural, it becomes *programmed*, and *invented* by technologies, to the extent that its disastrous effects happen to human beings, human affairs, and human systems and structures. The non-earthquake-resistant dwellings, schools, and masjids at Adassil in Morocco which turned to rubble in the 2023 earthquake invented the earthquake as accident, as disaster, and invented the people of Adassil as victims. In Tokyo, on the other hand, the Park Hyatt occupies floors thirty-eight to fifty-two in Japan's second tallest building. The tower is built to resist earthquakes. The tower invents and predicts the earthquake as disaster, too, but, though the Park Hyatt Tokyo sways above Tokyo in a terrifying way when the earthquake comes, it remains upright, it does not become rubble, and a thousand staff and guests are frightened and anxious but alive and probably uninjured unless an unexpectedly falling chandelier or flying shard of plate glass or heart attack, and so, at the moment of its design and construction, the Park Hyatt building invented the 2011 Tōhoku earthquake as disaster prevented for the safety of our privileged guests. At exactly the same time, the nuclear power plant built too-intimate with the seashore at Nahara invented the tsunami caused by the 2011 Tōhoku earthquake as disaster at the moment of its design and construction years before the natural wave towered in toward its reactors.

Worthy of the Event

"Read Paul Virilio, perhaps." I say to Norma Mapagu, who does not like it.

Well.

※

On a flight between Hà Nội and Paris, after three double Jack Daniels, no ice, and after refusing both beef and chicken, the man in the window seat tells me a story about the photographer, Võ Anh Ninh: In March 1945, Võ Anh Ninh packs a change of clothes, the man in the window seat says. There is great famine in the north; more than two million dead and dying, but still food in Hà Nội for people like Võ Anh Ninh. He packs a week's supply of bread and a dozen hard boiled duck eggs, not a lot, but more than the people he will see get to eat in two weeks, three, even, far more, Võ Anh Ninh knows. He packs his 1936 Zeiss Ikon Contaflex Twin lens Reflex camera and a dozen rolls of Fuji film. He would prefer Agfa, but the war in Europe. Võ Anh Ninh's usual subject is the beauties of Tonkin, Annam, even Cochin China when he gets an opportunity to go as far south as Sài Gòn,. he usually photographs rivers, and beaches, he dunes at Mũi Né and the ancient roofscapes of Hà Nội's precolonial quarter. And beautiful women. Võ Anh Ninh is an *art* photographer. But now he is photographing disaster. Later, Võ Anh Ninh will deny any political or even social objective, but when his photographs of famine in the north reach the people of Sài Gòn, who are not at all starving, his photographs become the slit eye of his camera through which the people of Sài Gòn *see* what and how Võ Anh Ninh's camera sees: two boys starving, already blind from no food, sitting by the seven-kilometer highway marker outside Thái Bình waiting to die, two of two million. The people of Sài Gòn see and *feel* as they imagine Võ Anh Ninh's Zeiss Ikon feels. They understand what they are looking at in the same way that Võ Anh Ninh's Zeiss Ikon understands what it is looking at, and the people of Sài Gòn know what they must do. They open their purses and food starts to flow north. But now, before the food from Sài Gòn arrives, Võ Anh Ninh is cycling north toward the border with China. On his blue Hirondelle, he treads the space between life and death in the town of Tiên Yên, silent, where he comes upon a woman wearing sunglasses waiting to die on the marble stoop of what he imagines is a merchant house near the river. Võ Anh Ninh offers the woman some bread and his second-last egg. She seems to smell it more than she sees it, and she takes it, no grabbing, and she thanks Võ Anh Ninh in French, and she eats the bread and the duck egg too quickly, he knows, and yes, she sicks it up, but as soon as it is out and in her lap and on the step, she gathers it up and eats it again. Võ Anh Ninh, takes about twenty-three pictures; these will be terrifying. But back in his darkroom in Hà Nội days later, when Võ Anh Ninh comes to the Tiên Yên roll of Fuji, it is as if a finger of light has lain itself on the film and the woman eating and vomiting and eating her vomit has been burned off. She is absent. Only the edges of the marble steps and something like the shadow of a hand remain to print. Useless Japanese rubbish, Võ Anh Ninh thinks. The man in the window seat presses the flight attendant call button. There is a twist of high air. The airplane jinks and flexes. I tell the man in the window seat I've read a lot about Võ Anh Ninh and never came across this story. The man in the window seat taps the left side of his nose and tells me he has *ins*.

※

In the summer of 2021, in the Irkutsk area of Siberia, the subarctic forests of Yakutia burned. Some say extreme summer temperatures caused by global heating were to blame for this great disaster; others say logging companies with Chinese contracts did it, or a confluence of global heating and habitat destruction for profit set the burning off. By the end of August, the blaze had incinerated an area of boreal forest larger than Portugal. Yet another northern hemisphere summer of fire, one might say, bored, there is so much of it every year, everywhere, what can be done, and even the catastrophic Portugal-sized reach and effects of the 2021 Yakutia fire failed to move most of us, unless our move was to mute the sound or find another channel or, if one is really a troublemaker, share on Facebook, Instagram, Twitter, or Telegram. The 2021 Yakutia fire was bigger than all the other fires burning in the world that same August, and there were many: California, Spain, Algeria, Greece, Türkiye, Canada, Oregon, Arizona, Northeast China. Toxic smoke from the burning Yakutia forest reached the

Arctic for the first time in recorded human history. Roza Dyachkovskaya tweeted: `Siberia is dying now.`

Roza Dyachkovskaya was wrong; we are all dying, we are all burning ourselves and our families and our friends and our enemies and our world to death. The technology of combustion invents the interminable end of it all. Or blame the trees for their bad habit of being combustible.

·

```
What is happening?
You might want to leave quicker.
There is this wind that sounds like 'phew,
phew, phew' like when you blow on a fire.
I can't breathe. Marie can't stop cough-
ing. It's close now.
Get in your car, now. Get in and drive.
It's ours now. I'm watching the house go
and the horses.
Heavenly Father, help us.
```
[3]

✺

John Hoskins, seaman: `Infamous Europeans, a scandal to the Christian name; is it you who bring and leave in a country with people you deem savages the most loathsome diseases?`

·

We colonizers find it hard to say we did it.

[3] From the Black Saturday bushfires in the Australian state of Victoria, February 7, 2009

Don't blame us for smallpox deaths in colonial Australia, we say; the evidence, we say, indicates the smallpox disaster began before *we* even got here. Smallpox, we say, was brought in from the Celebes by Makassans who visited the northwest Indian Ocean coast of the continent to collect trepang, which white Australians might call sea cucumber. From there, we say, smallpox traversed all that desert and all those grasslands and the not-easy mountain ranges between the Indian Ocean coast and the Pacific coast to reach in 1789 what is now Sydney, where it killed thousands and must have killed thousands as it made its way transcontinental. Some of us say that samples of smallpox-infected matter, variolas, were brought to the land by those first European settlers and either inadvertently or deliberately released onto the Dharug, Kuringgai and Dharawal peoples who are the rightful owners of what is now Sydney and its immediate areas and beyond, the whole continent. A Yorta Yorta man in a political philosophy class I taught said, "Those first white settlers gave us smallpox."

It was perfectly clear to him.

Over a couple of Mrs. Higa's very ono plate lunches with Spam, Rudy Rummel said the diseases brought to Oceania, Africa, and the Americas by European colonization killed at least one billion Indigenous people. Some estimate, Rudy Rummel said, that ninety percent of Indigenous Americans in what is now the mainland United States and Canada died because of diseases introduced by conquest and settlement. In the Caroline Islands, a smallpox epidemic killed almost half of the total population of five thousand in a single year: 1854. In Guam, one third of the Chamorro population died of smallpox in the island epidemic of 1856. David Stannard reckons that the population of the Hawaiian Islands was about eight-hundred and sixty thousand when James Cook visited in 1778. A century later, less than fifty thousand Hawaiians remained, killed mostly by smallpox but also tuberculosis, measles, venereal syphilis, chicken pox, and mumps.

I have read that smallpox in Australia killed approximately seventy percent of the total Aboriginal and Torres Strait Islander population in the one hundred and fifty years between that first epidemic in 1789 and when smallpox was brought under control in the twentieth century. The catastrophic burden of smallpox and all the other diseases caused by colonial destruction of traditional nutrition and traditional health sciences and culture itself continues in Australia even now. I don't know if those first generations of colonizers *planned* to use smallpox or measles or syphilis to wipe out populations, culture, whole civilizations, and thereby simplify dispossession, although planned infections did happen in North America, but I *do* know that settlers had a good understanding of how their presence would introduce new diseases to Indigenous peoples with catastrophic effects for Indigenous everything, and, while settler accounts of hideously blistered dead and dying Aboriginal adults and children were couched in a language of regret, the colonizers simultaneously argued that ```Only a race which has undergone evolution against the diseases of crowds is capable of civilization.```

On the disasters of modern colonialism, I've also read Aimé Césaire: ```They talk to me about progress,``` diseases cured, highways built, improved standards of living. I am talking about societies drained of their essence, cultures trampled underfoot, institutions undermined, lands confiscated, religions smashed, magnificent artistic creations destroyed, extraordinary possibilities wiped out.

I *understand* it – empire, colonialism, domination – yet even though I grew up right next to it and I saw the consequences, I saw the consequences without feeling the consequences. At some point, I learned to see the consequences, and know what I see, but seeing is not feeling, is it, and I don't *feel* it. I don't feel like a white settler in this place called Australia, but you know I am. I didn't *feel* like a haole all those years in Honolulu, so, when some tita or kanaka kepanī gave me you-haole eyes or threw me the bird and yelled fucking haole at me on H-1, I didn't get the message about my having and how my having entailed others not having. That not getting the message might be something to do with the not-having-ness of transsexual woman existence in most places where my privileges are as contingent as my beauties. But more than that, I don't get it because colonialism has not happened to me as disaster. I do not *feel* it.

Jedda yelled at me and Lana Luxemburg when we told her to take her business somewhere else, anywhere not here: "You fucking white queen queens think you're Captain fucking Cook. This is my fucking country, not yours."

Lana Luxemburg quoted Leon Trotsky at Jedda: `What is imperialism? It is the aspiration of capitalism to stop the existence of small governments`, and then she said something about how British imperialism in Australia is capitalism stopping the existence of Aboriginal traditions and lives, which even I knew was advanced for a girl from Bundaberg, terrible nose always in a book or not, Stalinist father or not, but then, always mercurial, Lana Luxemburg lost it, or the truth of Australia came out in her, and she screamed at Jedda, "Just fucking get out, get out, get out, you fucking b——g slag," and we both, Lana and I, ran at Jedda, who screamed **Bitches** and ran off into the grove of giant fig trees where it was dark and damp.

I don't *feel* any of it.

Even if I ask that Yorta Yorta man in the spring semester political philosophy class, how does it feel, the disaster of colonialism, and even if he *shows* me how it feels, I can't feel it. Even if I dare to say, "How does it feel to be invaded and put down?" to Jonathan Kamakawiwo'ole Osorio, and even if he condescends to answer in the break at that historiography seminar in Sakamaki Hall, I will be a disaster perv rubbernecking at a car crash on the freeway, watching *Air Disasters* on the Smithsonian Channel, imagining a man in the sea bitten in two by a great white shark, reading news about fires the size of Belgium turning the tundra to ash, and, oh, how glad I am I am not you, not me, I am not you, not me, not me, not here please, here I am feeling righteous at any Holocaust movie, television show, and novel, and don't forget what they did to girls somewhat like me in

Worthy of the Event

Hitler's Germany. Impertinent and prurient, my witness to the disaster will be, and there will be guilt and schadenfreude, there will be, and a kind of narcissism, there will be, so I don't ask, I don't say, I don't feel, and, in any case, even if I do feel, it is presumptuous to think the individual suffering conscience a matter of any consequence so I don't need to feel any of it, do I, but I *do wonder* how it feels.

•

The next time I saw Queen Liliuokalani to speak to was on the morning of the day she was vacating the Palace after surrendering her authority to the Provisional Government, January 18, 1893 at 11am. She was seated at the breakfast table, just about finishing. The Queen put her hands up to her forehead and leaned over for quite a little while without speaking to anyone, **she was overcome with grief, which of course we could not relieve.** On seeing me at the doorway the Queen said "*mai*." A familiar expression amongst Hawaiians bidding one to come and be welcome. As she gave me her hand when I reached the head of the table where she was sitting, I felt a slight tremor as I bent to kiss it. Her eyes were filled with tears. She motioned to me to sit beside her, which I did and it was as much as I could to restrain my own tears and emotion.

✳

We drink sake at dinner, and we are now a bit rollicking in a meticulous kind of way. O is trying hats again. She puts on what looks like a weimao in watered black silk taffeta with a red tassel from the crown and a red net veil from the brim. It is disastrous on O; it might be catastrophic on anyone. O says, "This is a ridiculous thing, isn't it."

She puts the twenty-first-century Okayama version of a Tang dynasty hat back on its stand. She walks her mini-Geiger counter around the hotel lobby, tick tick tick, but O is not focused on it, I see that.

She is readying herself for something, something which turns out to be a question she has for me, a question ripe enough for brown spots, rigid with thirty years of waiting and only outed now, I think, by the revelatory powers of the great disaster last month: "Was there some kind of childhood trouble that caused your change or were you just *cantankerous*? May I ask the question?"

Cantankerous is funny from O. She has considered cantankerous before saying it to me, I know. She has *chosen* cantankerous and practiced it. O intends cantankerous to be exact, but it is *not* exact at all, for I am *wild*, not cantankerous at all, and O's precise intention with cantankerous and the inexactness of the result of her cantankerous, makes me fall in love with O again, just for a minute, no more. "Ask me whatever, but use 'cantankerous' again, will you" I say, and then I say, "The truth is, the trouble came after."

Worthy of the Event

O is immediately, inexplicably mortified. She covers her mouth with her hand, she stuffs her little dosimeter in her bag, she uses very polite formal Japanese to apologize and rushes off to her room on the sixth floor.

•

```
The thing that breaks/us is all there is
sometimes
```

•

After: all there was, was stillness. How *still* it was after. Be still, they told me, or you'll ruin all Dr. Lendvay's lovely work, and I *was* still. How still it was when Mitchell called me a tabula rasa as he left after all of Dr. Lendvay's lovely work. How the apartment with the view of the golf course went still, still, still, still, still after Mitchell left, so still and so much still that all that stillness became *me*. Still there. Still here. Don't move. Wait for the stillness to take the whole city, still the land, still the island continent colony, still this breaking place, the world stilled, so still, it was. I had never been so stilled nor witnessed so much still; still, as still as stilled winter earth, not a worm moving, still like the carp upon the icy bottom of the winter frozen pond is still. All there was then was still, still, there in my still window, still in my bedroom in my stilled apartment waiting for my own future to appear now that the past had been abolished, stilled in the wait, not breaking, not anxious to go again, to unstill. Let me be still. "Fore!!!" the golfers shouted in the Rose Bay sun again and again the same, like a single clock stilled on four forever. How would they feel if a bomb exploded over the eighteenth hole, breaking them, turning them to vermilion spatter and their woods and irons and carts to cinders and molten metal, one final movement before still. How would they feel were a great wall of water to rush in through the heads of Sydney Harbour and break upon them, stilling them, still all their already stilled dreams forever.

"But it was what you wanted, wasn't it?" O says two days later, me driving, and she, turning her little Geiger counter toward the poisoned sea.

```
The cyclones spin/ but I /hear nothing but
silence
```

※

Fairy's disaster is never previous nor even happening now. Fairy's disaster is a future that never happens but always requires **run!** Papa and Mama raised Fairy to believe that her disaster lies forever somewhere ahead. Fairy's mother and Fairy's father also raised Fairy on the story that she is the embodiment of disaster averted: You almost nearly not quite, we were terrified, died because of infantile bronchitis or pneumonia or whooping cough, which one is never clear, they told Fairy over and over and over again, they still do, they are so repetitive, and the disaster averted became part of who Fairy is and who she could be, for the disaster averted may yet come. She is forever trying to avoid it, **run!**

    I am not sure it is any of my business, still, I do wonder if Fairy's future disaster might be nothing to do with her, the future of her lungs, but everything to do with a past

Worthy of the Event

disaster not averted about which almost all goes unspoken. I wonder if Fairy's *past* disaster might be the father who still murmurs `beautiful girl` and licks his lips at the sight of forty-year-old Fairy eating her breakfast pretzel and Weißwurst at the dining room table. There is a Fairy story there I am not worthy to tell. I am too close to Fairy for it, even now, so far and long apart, and Fairy always says, "It didn't feel bad. I don't feel bad." She doesn't want to be reduced to trauma; well, who does, except memoirists, but are *didn't hurt* and *doesn't hurt* worthy of Fairy's before event, whatever it was? In the meantime, pestilence is always coming for Fairy. This might be love: **run!** She fights the futuristic disaster that may be pouring from the air nozzles of airliners and long-distance buses, and if she can't turn the air nozzles off, Fairy shrouds her poor little head in sweaters, wraps, up with the hoodie if she has one, and looks at the floor all the way from Doha to Singapore, Istanbul to Munich. **Run!** What might happen to those girly lungs is the only disaster Fairy can ever see. She says when kissing me, "Don't hold your breath, darling, this is not a disaster, this is *kissing*, don't be afraid," and I want to say, I am not afraid. I am trying to be worthy of it.

※

Disaster lengthens the distance between what is done and how what is done is done. In that length, questions form and appear, and in that distance, `ruin becomes the condition of change.` You wouldn't think the crash of JL123 into a Gunma mountain ridge and the death of almost all on board would be much more than a painful blip in Japan where there is a society that might be thought inured to disaster, so many delivered and received: conquest and colonialism; military rule and total war; the fire-bombing of Tokyo; the nuclear bomb attacks on Hiroshima and Nagasaki; great earthquakes in great abundance; tsunami; volcanic eruptions; landslides sweep entire communities away; toxic pollution events; sarin gas in the Tokyo subway; typhoons. Yet the crash of JL123 gouged Japan, and that gouge endures even now. The JL123 disaster did what all disasters and accidents have the potential to do: it changed the way people thought about systems, entities, formal and informal relationships, about governance, and the rules. Japan Airlines and Boeing, previously and almost universally admired in Japan, lost the trust of the public and of the government. People saw a new and disturbing discrepancy between government safety laws, rules, and the administration and implementation of them. They wondered if lives could be safely entrusted.

For some, the past became the now. New tissue formed around the wounds. Every August 12th, Japan's television networks show new documentaries about the crash and why it happened and what was done and not done about it happening. Almost every August 12th, new articles or new books appear examining the crash again, relitigating, finding new explanations and blame for it. Every August 12th, no matter how sweltering the day, many, many people make a pilgrimage to the crash site and to Uenomura village down in the valley, not the families of the JL123 dead so much, but people seeking a way to distance themselves from the rush and clamor of daily life and to quiet their minds through contemplation of disaster, the transience of all things, the beauties of survival.

※

We wonder about Miss Sybil Fontaine. Big Denise tells me she died of metastatic anal cancer in 1990. We wonder what might have become of Miss Sybil Fontaine's suit that could have been Chanel, but was not, her overcoat that might have been Aquascutum but was not, the hats that could have been hats from Manhattan milliners but were not. Are Miss Sybil Fontaine's beautifully kept hands, Miss Sybil Fontaine's beautiful lips nothing but ash now or turned to jerky all dry and stringy like the lips of an Egyptian mummy? I would meditate upon what is left of Miss Sybil Fontaine, were I not afraid she might raise up her carcass and advance upon me saying from tatters of cruel Dior Trans-Siberian-Express-red lips (real) in a full upper bow, also real, "Get the fuck off this corner. It's mine, it's always been mine. It's mine until I say it's not mine. Get off now or I'll flatten you."

We wonder about ourselves: I am me, more beautiful to myself than ever before, I am, but Big Denise is no longer Big Denise, not even Denise anymore, but another name, and no longer big, and each time I see her, every ten years or so, I ask myself, why Big? She is not big at all. No-longer-Big-Denise-or-even-Denise is now another person, really, one who accepts any and all pronouns in any order and lives in an old house with a steep orange roof and a view of the Baltic Sea on a sandy lane on Hiddensee, the island where Käthe Kollwitz spent a summer or two after the Gestapo visited her in Berlin in 1936 and threatened to send her and Karl to one of those concentration camps but did not because Käthe Kollwitz by then was a bit too famous, or there was something lucky for her and Karl. Not too long ago, no-longer-Big-Denise-or-even-Denise and I had coffee and cake at SchmuckBar in Kloster, and no-longer-Big-Denise-or-even-Denise told me that cisgender people use trans people to produce man and woman, much like slave-owners used enslaved people to produce master and mistress: fundamental units of the machine. "Old Sybil was right. What a fucking disaster when you think about it. That's how it *feels*, it feels as though it was all catastrophic. I refuse to exist for *them*, which is why I live out here where nobody sees me, and if they do, I pretend I don't speak a word, where it is just me and the dog and the gulls and the beach and a weekend in Berlin for the shops and Staatsoper. It seems to me, sometimes, that in the name of liberation to be our authentic selves, we have become more dependent and enslaved than ever, inauthentic."

And no-longer-Big-Denise-or-even-Denise is right, it is that easy, but it is not that easy, she is also not right, and it is right to be right and not right at the same time in the same place about the same thing, for one of the ways to be worthy of what happens is to make or let things be both right and wrong at the same time. One of the endowments of any long survival of any kind and any intensity of disaster might be the ability to hold usually mutually antagonistic values and concepts together with love. I look at no-longer-Big-Denise-or-even-Denise and her home with its view of the Baltic Sea and the perfectly-controlled lyrical poems she publishes in perfect German and the books she reads and her autonomy, and I know how hurt she has been, how ruined; I know her disasters, how worthy of her events she has been, and I think how no-longer-Big-Denise-or-even-Denise has become another person, untouchable no matter how touched.

"We are antifragile, darling," she says.

I could ask what antifragile is exactly except I do not want to look stupid in front of no-longer-Big-Denise-or-even-Denise so I remain unknowing about antifragile until I get back to Google and to the high flat near Schillerplatz and my view of the River Elbe, and when I finally understand Nassim Nicholas Taleb and antifragility, I think no-longer-Big-Denise-or-even-Denise would have more chance with prayer to the gods or the powers of her choice, some metaphysic, than with turning investment banking into philosophy.

※

That Marquês de Pombal in Lisbon after the 1755 earthquake: what a man. He was not fragile. He had Lisbon redesigned and rebuilt so that it was elegant, had modern transportation, trash collection, and sewage. All new buildings were built to a code designed to withstand the next earthquake, slow down the spread of fire, and make it easier for people to evacuate. Very scientific, but I'm betting that Marquês de Pombal also did a few rosaries every Sunday in one of the rebuilt cathedrals praying, oh, please, Holy Father, let this be enough and, oh, God don't let it come again too soon (he knew for sure never was too much to ask).

•

Harry DMs me: The one-hundred-and-fifty-year-old banyan tree at Lahaina is putting out leaves now after that terrible fire. Can trees be worthy of the event?

•

L cannot quite rid herself of the shock of disaster. She has tried `raising a glass in her season of ash` but defiance and even the art of celebration burned off in the car crash. L is still afraid of riding in a speeding car, yet, even as she clutches her throat and the handgrip, slow down, for fuck's sake, there is a kind of transcendence streaming off L like ribbons you want to catch for yourself. The shock of her disaster has imprisoned L in dregs of her experience, looking for it to come again, yet the accident also distanced L from all the usual rules about everything. She has grown and ennobled. Fear makes L beautifully interested in survival, in life anyway, but ugly in her methods: for L now, everything is economics, but in the night with brushtail possums rampaging on her roof, L still tries a metaphysic, does a few Hail Marys and please, Holy Mother, never again, I pray.

•

Worthy of the Event

After the disaster of brutal war and defeat in what is known now as King Philip's War or the First Indian War or the Great Narragansett War or Metacom's Rebellion the Native Americans of the places now known as Rhode Island, eastern Massachusetts and Connecticut, and coastal Maine, showed signs of compliant prayer to the God of the Puritans, imploring, the settlers often thought, His forgiveness for the sins of resistance and pleading for no more catastrophic violence. What the Puritan settlers could not or would not see was the Indian peoples of New England arming their lives with a metaphysic, not prayerful at all, and designed to keep their Indigenous cosmology intact and distinct. New England Indian people's dreams and dream meanings, language and symbology survived all the disasters of settlement, if not intact, certainly enough to stage the great resurgences of Native American cultures starting in the 1920s and continuing now.

•

The settlers on Wiradjuri country in inland south-eastern Australia called this lovely place by the river, Wellington Valley, and they called Mooinba, Gentleman Jacky. The settlers also brought smallpox. In the first three years of the 1830s up to one third of the Wiradjuri people in the Wellington Valley died; the virus struck them down numerously and almost without exception. Mooinba organized a metaphysic, which might have been, in Wiradjuri terms, a kind of prayerful metaphysic. He created a new form of Baiame waganna: a dance for, about, and materializing the creator and sky father of Wiradjuri people. Mooinba's new Baiame waganna was both a kind of plea to the Wiradjuri cosmos and the re-arming of Mooinba's people with new weapons, metaphysical though not metaphysical in the way that metaphysical sometimes means after physical, since I've read that Wiradjuri people do not cleave the divine and the world. That Mooinba died shortly thereafter, and that his retooling of a Wiradjuri metaphysic failed to send white settlers to hell and keep country in the hands of traditional guardians/owners should not be seen as a failure of Wiradjuri metaphysics, for Mooinba's Baiame waganna might be one of the things that has kept Wiradjuri peoples alive and fighting through disaster after disaster, two centuries of it, to keep and reclaim country yesterday, now, tomorrow.

※

They asked Gertrude Stein what she thought of the atomic bomb. She told them she had not been able to take any interest in it she liked to read detective and mystery stories but whenever the detective and mystery stories had death rays or atomic bombs in them, no. All that destruction was not interesting to Gertrude Stein it was the living that interested Gertrude Stein not death and destruction perhaps people were interested in the atomic bomb because they are scared of the atomic bomb but Gertrude Stein was not so scared, there is so much to be scared of so what is the use of bothering to be scared, and if you are not scared the atomic bomb is not interesting. This is

Worthy of the Event

`a nice story`. Gertrude Stein was not in need of any metaphysic except Alice; she had no need to pray, except to Alice. She needed no help except herself and Alice against the terrors of human existence.

✳

On the last day but one, I read a newspaper story about the hairstylist up in Fukushima doing his wife's hair one last time in the giant morgue where she now lies after extraction from great wet pillows of mud down the coast near Sendai. O takes me to a lunch of salt-grilled ayu just caught from the fast Maze River, first of the season, and O's little Geiger counter stays in her purse and mute for most of the day. After ayu, we hike in our lady shoes up an almost vertical mountain slope above the valley, up, up, up in the dry shadows of cedar trees we go until we come, panting, and me red, to a tiny white dragon shrine in a mossy grove at the base of the waterfall. O does not wash her hands nor rinse her mouth. There is no bow, nor does she jingle the suzu bells. O does not offer ¥5 to the white dragon god of the waterfall; she gives nothing, not even one of the Lotte Black Black Tablet Strong Type breath mints she always keeps in her purse. "You always," I say, "Why not now?"

O says she no longer prays. "I am a convert to the religion of the future," she says, though Roberto Mangabeira Unger's *Religion of the Future* is still in the future, or my memory might be wrong, and what O says might be she no longer implores the gods because religion is not the future. I don't know, but we sit and watch the white dragon cascade and roar straight down into the pool at the base of the cliff, bursting into spray and rainbows and diamonds, and we talk about human beings becoming less attached to abstraction and heavenly omnipotence, less hopeful of transcending the world. We talk about human beings becoming more divine, deeply free, free enough to pray to ourselves when things fall apart. I tell O about Miss Sybil Fontaine and her predictions. O talks about seeing the present as based on the future rather than the past. She talks about a religion requiring us to live for tomorrow, next year, next century, next millennium, the year 4051. Let us begin to live as beings uncontained by the circumstances of our existence, and no matter how hard, how terrifying our disasters and our loves, let us be people who do not need and do not seek heavenly consolations.

O takes out the little Geiger counter, turns it on, and reads the screen. "We are safe enough here now," she says.

"This is the world that must be endured," I say.

O says, "Or these are the events of which we must be worthy."

VI: stardust

Infinity is now my concern.
One of my cousins sometimes fainted. Dr. Wickramasinghe thought being born blue with the cord in a stranglehold around the neck and touch and go for weeks was behind the boy's syncope, and "He will grow out of it."

My aunt agreed that the fainting spells had something to do with her baby coming out pretty much dead, but she also thought that, at some point in his passage from her womb, the infant had gone through a door between two dimensions or two worlds, between here and there, between mortals and angels, and he was still going there and back at the age of fourteen; perhaps growing out of it was yet to come. Sometimes my cousin came back from a faint or whatever it was and told his mother about beautiful lights and being in a place where "I saw everything," but Dr Wickramasinghe said, "That is only prodromal phenomena."

A week after my cousin's fifteenth birthday, the first real frost white as salt on the morning lawn and all of us waiting unwilling and shivering for the school bus, my cousin fainted and never came back and later his mother thought, My baby knows everything now, all the time.

See my sister and the girls turning and whirling and spinning themselves around and around like happy tops, ten thousand revolutions, and giggling until the centrifuge effect kicks in and the giggles stop, and the girls twirl silent now, serious in the sinking, flaming bars of the autumn sunset. The girls turn on grass already pearled with dew. They become dizzy, they feel sick, they collapse and say, "Where am I?" or "Everything is spinning," and one of the twins vomits Easter chocolate onto her pinafore. The girls turn. They whirl, spinning around and around and around and around, almost vanishing to themselves. My sister opens her eyes and looks right through me. She weaves across the grass. "I saw black stars in the sky," she says, and turns again in the indigo dusk. Venus grinds to a halt in the heavens. Time itself hangs idle from the smooth arms of red gum trees, and yet, five-fifteen becomes five-twenty in exactly five minutes, and Aunty Snow yells from the bright oblong of the kitchen window "Dinner, you lot!" and the girls stop turning, they pull back from what might have become an irreversible disappearance into something dreadful or wondrous, surely unknown, and they go inside, where, presented with Heinz spaghetti on toast and a grilled sausage, they don't feel much like eating.

The girls, turning, are dancing. The girls, dancing, refigure the movements of celestial bodies, woozy orbits and nauseating revolutions around and around again, circling toward some dimension on the far side of syncope. Their dance comes from the heart of human being. The girls' turning owes something to a certain human way of being, to Iberian fertility dances, to the entrancing horse dances of Java, maypole dances, the embodied disembodiment of dhamaal, that beating, spinning choreography which transports persecuted Sufi mystics and Muslims and Hindus stuck forever in the slums and shantytowns of Sind and Punjab toward God until they faint, maste qalandar! The dance of the twirling girls is like the crazy Shrovetide carnival dances Christians used to do. The girls' turning dance is a folía, a little madness, a folly, non-liturgical but brimming with belief. It is a relative of the swooning waltz. You can hear it even in the stately proportions of Baroque. Listen. Listen to Arcangelo Corelli's Violin Sonata in D Minor, op. 5, no. 12 ("La Folia"): adagio progression gives way to violins spiraling faster and faster, twirling on and on through twenty-three variations of the original chords until, not frenzy, but a deliberate and organized ecstatic pattern takes over. The girls turning might be as old as human life itself, around and around until you collapse or rise, and things go black.

In bed that night, my sister hyperventilates. Our mother enters, soft. She hands my sister a tiny medicine glass half full of warm water stained with tobacco-colored drops of Chlorodyne, which, in 1958, is not yet considered addictive even though its principal ingredient is tincture of opium, and too much can send you right into a black star or permanently oblique like Mrs. Moller in the red brick corner house whose regime of Rothman's cigarettes and Chlorodyne turned her into an unmoving sage given to utterances like, "You are not meant to be here," her eyes permanently focused somewhere else. Chlorodyne is a chemical version of the turning dance. It induces a kind of syncope. It makes the lights smear and go out, it takes you somewhere, and it bears my sister down a darkening slope into silence. Going, she says, "When I was turning, I saw Dad in Heaven. It was all black, not like they say, golden," and then she's gone and the night on the farm is at last still but for the song of an insomniac Willie Wagtail floating up to the house from the creek paddock and that resentful susurration all burgled country makes, get out, get out, get out. I get up in the dark and find the bottle of Chlorodyne in Aunty Snow's bathroom cupboard. I squeeze three drops onto my tongue, that anise flavoring, and faint away.

※

Effects of Opium

```
We cannot withhold the record of an extra-
ordinary case of delusion, occasioned by
an opiate, in the person of a gentleman
with whom we have the pleasure of being
most intimately acquainted. To relieve a
laryngeal cough with which he was troubled,
he sucked, one night, prior to going to
bed, a few morphia lozenges, he could
not exactly say how many. He remembered
```

to have retired and undressed himself as usual, and to have attended to all the particulars of the toilet, in which he was especially neat; for, though a plain man, he had all the vanity of a handsome one. He placed his night-lamp on the mantel, and got into bed. He lay looking, as was his wont, at the taper, until it became slowly surrounded by a halo of thinnest mist, which gradually filled the whole room. At the same time he felt himself growing by degrees lighter, until at last he fancied himself to float upon the very wings of ether. He could move in any direction, and variously tried the action of his limbs, but every effort gave him a further and more fertile idea of his imponderosity. Shortly, the notion possessed him his head was off. (*Scientific American*, Vol. 3, No. 11, December 4, 1847, p. 86)

※

What do the girls, turning, see and feel, and where are they trying to go? Do they lose their heads and come upon their own *imponderosity* or are their turning experiences cinematic in the way that Antonin Artaud meant cinematic: a total reversal of values; a complete disruption of optics, perspective, and logic; an ecstatic condition that is almost, but not quite, another dimension altogether in which the girls do not exist *there* and also do not quite exist *here* on the farm on that Easter Sunday evening. Gone but not gone, turning away the girls are, like Harry, who went through a time when he spent hours almost every day in one of those flotation tanks. "It is not like Vipassana sitting," he said, "which brings you to yourself. Flotation takes me away somewhere, it is water, but it could be the sky, another world."

How Harry felt about flotation is how *I* once felt about pills, working in hospitals and every kind of narcotic and sleeping drug right there, ten thousand tickets to some other side: great brown jars of white, scarlet, purple, royal blue, green-and-black, candy-pink pills and caps; hypnotics and barbiturates lined up on white shelves, one for the patient, two for me and later. On my days off, I swallowed pills in even numbers, four, six, even eight, and then, after I read somewhere, perhaps in Mishima Yukio's novels, that odd numbers are preferred in Japan, where I had never gone then but intended, I took five, seven, nine, sometimes only three, and went to bed to seek what I thought of as **The Void**.

Sometimes I went so far out I almost made a landing and stayed away so long that I, or a.k.a. Victor Mature, whoever was with me in those times began to worry, she's dead, she's trying to kill herself, she is *so* damaged by all that tranny stuff, call an ambulance, but I was not damaged, or not damaged enough to seek death, I was turning, I was fainting for answers, not to the unanswerable question incessantly put to trans people – What the fuck are you? – which is another story and not for here, no, I wanted to know what was possible. I wanted a glimpse of other worlds, other dimensions, the fifth dimension at least, which Oskar Klein thought too lightless and too small to be visible to the human eye and probably curling in upon itself like an infinitesimal armadillo at the approach of strange matter. Give me the sixth, seventh, and eighth dimensions, where, according to string theory, one may traverse the planes of *possibilities* and witness every permutation of what *can* occur in multiple futures and what *could* have occurred in multiple pasts. Let me see, just a glimpse, come on, give me the ninth dimension where all universal laws of physics and the conditions in each universe become apparent, how wonderful, and admit me, plus one if you like, but I will pay, to that ultimate dimension, what must surely be the real Heaven, the tenth dimension, where everything becomes possible and imaginable.

※

My father's dead name is Schrödinger: he is at once deceased and present, gone, not gone, in two dimensions or states or worlds or places at the same time. The not-gone my father may dwell in one of those string-theoretical dimensions between five and ten. There, he goes on forever as a dark-particle version of who he *is* (not *was* in my world) before he runs his MG roadster into a telephone pole on the road from Nowra; who he *is* before the impact tosses him onto a field of emerald grass where he lies with a jutty of brain matter poking from a crack in his skull, and the Friesian cows, who are often terrible busybodies, rest their cuds for a moment and make elaborate cow eyes at the accident, and briny mist drifts in from where the Tasman Sea bludgeons the beach, foaming almost to the sandy toes of dunes covered in thickets of banksia and pigface: dead on arrival, and the death unlikely to have been lyrical for my father. My mother decides not to tell me of my father's death. She says, "The child is so young and can't possibly understand it, what is the point, Christmas is just around the corner."

Nor am I allowed at my father's funeral, the cremation, his ashes cast into Botany Bay. I am parked at the house of Great-Aunt Clarice Willoughby, who writes bodice-rippers and has always doubted my parents' marriage and is happy to stay at home with the child, a glass of Amontillado, and a pack of Tarot cards. She says she saw this coming, look, The Tower. I already prefer The World with its image of a naked woman, pink and floating above the planet, and The World is close to what I finally get.

Almost seventy years after, when the night does not move and the Southern Cross stands above the downtown teeth of this city, I hear my father's little car stuttering outside the house. He has travelled from wherever dimension, whatever world, to be with me. I feel his eyes *on* me like fingers through the glass, and there is the perfume of father, which is the smell of salt and ozone and fresh wood shavings and dust and eucalyptus and avgas and, unaccountably, anise. My father is there but he cannot speak to me. I cannot see him, yet I feel him, can he feel me? His little car putters; his scents twirl on the night air. He comes from some enigmatic *where*, but has he come bearing messages from another dimension or are these encounters with my father only instances of what Maria Török says is the fixated child's unwavering hope that one day the object will once again be what it was in the privileged moment? I don't know.

※

I am flying into the unknown, Jean-Marie Saget tells *France-Soir* before he climbs into the cockpit of the Dassault Mirage 4000 twinjet fighter aircraft prototype, I am going to the other side! There is some chance Saget may not return from the unknown, but in the end it is the Mirage 4000 itself which vanishes forever into obscurity since the only serious order for the type comes from the Kingdom of Saudi Arabia, and Saudi Arabia cancels its order when the United Kingdom agrees to accept oil as payment for a fleet of British Aerospace Tornado fighter jets, and the single Mirage 4000 prototype which had taken Jean-Marie Saget to the other side is turned into a Dualit toaster, or something else shiny. Maybe my father simply flew too far to the other side to properly return and that is what death is: too far to come back as yourself, I don't know, but I *do* know that Martin Heidegger knew that no matter how close to death you get, the living cannot be more than *alongside* the deaths of others. Maybe what death is, is not important. Who cares if death is not on Google Maps? Gone is gone even when gone is not gone in some part of me or not gone in some other place I've yet to know.

✳

I have had more anesthetics than most people, and you know why. Anesthetics: I like them all. I like propofol thiopental etomidate sevoflurane isoflurane desflurane fospropofol. I like all anesthetics because I wake up more beautiful after anesthetic, or I wake up healthier, or both beautiful and healthy – are they not the same thing. "Dribble it in slowly," I say to whoever anesthesiologist, which usually gets a laugh and very slow but sometimes a little savagery and pushing the anesthetic in so fast it hurts enough to make me cry out for a millisecond until I am gone into that other dimension, which I used to think of as just another version of the Seconal-dead-drunk-rohypnol-out-of-it other dimension but which may be something quantum. A group of University of Michigan scientists found functional quantum properties in the state of unconsciousness brought on by various ether-based anesthetics. Halogenated ethers interact with entangled photons, the University of Michigan scientists say. This result motivates further studies on the possible quantum interactions that anesthetic molecules may have in the brain and the atomic or subatomic particles they may be targeting; The Michigan research does *not* show that quantum interactions spin me into another dimension when I am anesthetized and out on the table, the scorched scent of bleeders sealed up with heat filling the clinical air, or a camera up my ass, but I do wonder about Michael Jackson's many sessions with propofol and whether he was visiting other worlds and other dimensions where he was not thought to be guilty or innocent of something, where what he had had done to his face was unworthy of remark, where nobody thinks it is horrific to dangle an infant from a hotel window. If alternate worlds and universes are infinite, there might be one like that.

✺

Fairy consults some Moroccan shaman in Switzerland. She returns from some suburb of Basel to tell me that losing a parent so young is like some train accident. The locomotive slams into an oncoming train. The collision sets off a chain of damage as the carriages behind collide horrendously into one another, bang, bang, bang, bang, bang across time and generations. "You have been reading Sigrid Weigel," I say, "that télescopage stuff."

Fairy looks at me with oceanic eyes and tender like she sometimes is, and she says, "Not that, only that nothing ends, and I've heard you crying over that Luther Vandross song about fathers and mothers," and she is right, that Luther Vandross song sung by Luther Vandross never Celine Dion does make me cry. And Fairy is wrong. Every *life* and every *thing* does end or at least passes into transubstantiation. It is only dimensionality that is eternal. Time and what time contain do not end, and all times are equally real: December 13, 1954, my father alive and making clever jokes; December 14, 1954, my father turned an injured lilac color on a steel table at the morgue. Then might be as real now as it was then.

※

I'm in a club near Calle Hamburgo at three in the morning with Cuauhtémoc (family names withheld). His lips come close to my left ear. I could die happy. We are working through thirteen different mezcals drawn from bottles lined up on the glittering bar. I've been down in San Cristóbal de las Casas for three months about a year after the Zapatista rebellion and everybody in Chiapas holding their breath, especially the Maya people, who wait to be punished by the state as they have usually been punished by the state. In the mornings, mist from distant cloud forest fingers the zocalo, and the days are short and cold at that elevation. I grow afraid of something or nothing; so fearful do I grow I exercise my privilege and fly away and go to this club in the Zona Rosa where Cuauhtémoc's lips are on my ear now, heading south, as soft as warm feathers, don't stop there, and he tells me we live in a kind of cosmic painting. "Everything is teotl," he says and a lot more I don't understand then or even now, but much later, when I am back in the Green Mountains and snow falling in sheets outside the windows of the library, I read:

Worthy of the Event

There are no absolute beginnings — or absolute endings, for that matter — in Aztec metaphysics. There are only continuings. Death, for example, is not an ending but a change of status, as that which dies flows into and feeds that which lives. All things are involved in a single, never-ending process of recycling and transformation. There is furthermore no time prior to or after teotl since time is defined wholly in terms of teotl's becoming. Nor is there space outside of teotl since space, too, is defined wholly in terms of teotl's becoming. I take this to mean that in some way I fail to properly understand, all times and all spaces – the fifth, sixth, seventh, eighth, ninth, and tenth dimensions, here, there, then, now, tomorrow, that black hole – exist as themselves and exist also at a point at which their particular temporal and spatial distinctions vanish. The mask makers of Tlatilco and Oaxaca sell double-faced masks, one half a living face, the other a skull. There is no opposition in them, however, no alive versus dead, no good against evil. Although death, life, good, and evil are present in the two-faced masks of Tlatilco and Oaxaca, they are teotl; death and life and good and evil do not exist in polarity to one another but in a kind of swirling rotation, a teotlizing that spins us all into wisdom.

✷

The Story of Kim Soon Ae, formerly known as Mariam Johari

On a steaming day of the 1943 monsoon season in the second year of the Japanese occupation, in what is now that part of Malaysia just across from Singapore, three soldiers of the Japanese Southern Army grab Mariam Johari from the fruit stall in the market at Plentong where she sells durian, jackfruit, rambutan, mangosteen, little sugary bananas, star fruit as yellow as lemons but sweet, and anything else she can get. The soldiers put Mariam Johari and her fruit, except the durian

 [Well, maybe the durian went in too, for durian fetor can make anybody drool for the paradisical sweet within, and also, in that war, food was food]

into the back of a wheezing Nissan 180 truck where there are already a dozen other young women

 [she says in 2007]

most of them local Teochow and Hakka Chinese, but three Malays. Mariam Johari makes four. She is gone.

 [According to Mariam Johari's three children]

The abduction itself goes unmentioned by the grandparents with whom the three children now live. The grandparents might dread to speak of Mariam Johari at all for fear that the neighbors and the kampung imam may say she has gone to *fornicate* with Japanese kafir, which is a terrible sin even if the fornication is without consent. For the children, it might be as though their mother has gone to another dimension, another world, and after a few weeks, they don't even look along the lane which skirts the rubber trees to see if she might be coming home

Worthy of the Event

[As elderly adults, the children talk publicly about how their mother seemed to have gone somewhere unknowable]
and come home their mother eventually does, appearing in the rain of another monsoon in November 1945 like a visitor from a distant planet,
[maybe]
her hair uncovered, marcelled, wearing a Chinese style dress of peacock blue satin, lips as spiked and as red as the husks of lychees, and something has happened to her eyebrows.
[I am imagining here although not the eyebrows, which appear, thin and painted into high arches, in a snapshot of Kim-Soon-Ae-formerly-known-as-Mariam-Johari taken around that time]
Mariam Johari reappears to her children in the company of a young soldier wearing a Japanese uniform stripped of insignia. "He is *not* Japanese," she tells her father, "But *Korean*."

This means nothing good to the father. He turns his face away and leaves the veranda without speaking. The Korean soldier offers candies to the children, who stick them into their mouths and suck them silently and watch Mariam Johari have a conversation in hisses with her mother, whose message seems to be you can't stay, they are killing women who *did things* with the Japanese, you had better go away, which was the usual urgent message given to Malay and Teochow and Hakka Chinese women suspected of consorting with the Japanese when they tried to come home after the war ended. "I am going away," Mariam Johari says to her children. She tells them that she will return with coconut butter biscuits

[The son has a distinct memory of what kind of cookie his mother promised]
and then she is gone.

The children wait for their mother to appear again. They wait until they are adults and parents themselves with houses and mangosteen trees of their own near Kota Tinggi, not far from the tomb of Sultan Mahmud II at Kampung Makam, Village of Tombs. The children wait for their mother and the coconut butter cookies until they are grandparents and old, and still their mother does not return, nor any letter, well, she can't read or write, but no message passes from mouth to mouth either. When it comes up, they say, "Oh, our mother is dead, the war," but they don't mean it. They hope, they wonder if their mother has removed to somewhere unimaginable and unknowable and in that other world their mother might now be somebody or something else.

["Always," says the son]

He sees a news story on 8TV about a Korean Broadcasting System television producer from Seoul who is in Singapore looking for the children of Mariam Johari. The son calls the number on the screen and within a couple of weeks the children, who are now grandparents, are in Seoul where they have two reunions with an old Korean woman called Kim Soon Ae who wears traditional Korean dresses shaped like bells and is also, apparently, their mother. The first reunion is almost intimate in the green room at KBS studios.

[I have no information about what transpired there except there were tears, although not from the eyes of Kim Soon Ae]

Worthy of the Event

The second reunion occurs under lights and before cameras on the set of *Love in Asia*, a popular television series about romances between Koreans and foreigners. "Come home now, ibu," they say to Kim Soon Ae who is also their mother, but she doesn't seem to understand Bahasa Malay, and she has a Korean son, a Korean grandchild, and nobody in Seoul refers to her as Mariam Johari, it's only Kim Soon Ae.

Yet, this little old Korean woman *is* their mother, and they argue and plead. The government and religious authorities of the state of Johor plead, and the national government in Kuala Lumpur adopts a faintly threatening tone for if Kim Soon Ae returns in time for the fiftieth anniversary of the Malaysian state, that would be ideal. But she will not come then for them, and she waits until the fiftieth birthday of the nation is over, then she comes, Kim Soon Ae comes to Kota Tinggi as Mariam Johari in a great circus of publicity for the Korean television network and for the fiftieth anniversary of Malaysia even though it was a month or more ago.

She stays a couple of weeks. The children who are now grandparents tell the television and newspapers how happy they are to have their mother back. She is *home* now. But even arrayed in a turquoise hijab, the woman who is their mother seems like matter out of place. There is a rumor that she cannot manage a single enunciation of the Shahada: `There is no God but Allah and Muhammad is the Messenger of Allah`. Even worse, she wants to go home. She does not want to stay here, and she tells her children and grandchildren through a translator that the place is bad for her health, and she disappears again, although the children know now where it is she goes in late September 2007. Mother is not *here*.

Two years later, Kim Soon Ae who used to be Mariam Johari dies in Seoul. She leaves detailed instructions about what to do with her remains and how to do it, but even so, an ugly fight breaks out over where her remains should be and did she die a Muslim or a Christian? Her Korean son surrenders to the Malaysian son and Kim Soon Ae becomes Mariam Johari again, one last time and she comes back from another world to her children *here* who are now grandparents, and her embalmed remains are buried in the red dirt behind the masjid where Sultan Mahmud II is entombed, not too far from where the children live.

[The wife of the imam of the masjid where Sultan Mahmud II is entombed told me the old children sometimes tottered down the road with their arms full of red and yellow heliconia spears for their mother's grave, which I could not find when I went there, she was still not *here,* for me, at least, and I imagined her son and daughter, every day looking in the mirror for their mother but seeing only their own old, sad faces. The imam's wife knew the whole story, she thought, she said, and she told me that this world, those other places that might not be places at all, her love for her own baby boy, the grief of those poor old children, it is all one God.]

※

My concern now is the future infinite.

`This world was meant to bend`, says the Igbo spirit within Ada's body in Akwaeke Emezi's *Freshwater*, but only great mass and perhaps great kinetics can make "this world" bend into a curve steep enough to allow movement between here and other dimensions, parallel universes, mirror worlds. We owe much of the unfailingly popular theory of multiple worlds to the American physicist Hugh Everett III, who suggested that beyond the physical realities we can observe, the entire universe may be described by a gigantic wave function holding within it all possible realities, including two realities in the future unraveled from one reality, and two more realities unraveled from the two unraveled realities and so on until multiple worlds appear. In the multiverse hypothesis, the universe is everything and infinite, but the universe is also only what *we* can see, so there may be other Big Bangs than our own Big Bang, other universes than our own universe.

Andrei Linde talks about endless universes squeezing and popping out of each other like bubbles in a chaotic and eternal inflation of universes, each with its own laws of physics. Richard Feynman made diagrams of all the possible outcomes of electromagnetic interactions between electrons and photons. These Feynman diagrams have ten thousand uses. They also suggest that there may be millions, maybe endless, trajectories toward millions, maybe endless realities (outcomes), and only the most probable trajectory, usually the shortest, gets to the universe you and I know as real. Some other outcomes might be M- (for mirror) worlds, as opposed to the O- (for original) world where we are now. M-worlds may seem to be the stuff of science fiction like the clever television series *Counterpart*, but they are a formal hypothesis of quantum mechanics. In *Counterpart*, a passage opens between O-world Berlin and the M-world Berlin. The drama begins in that opening. In the mirror worlds hypothesis, the mirror (M) and the original (O) worlds are symmetrical except perhaps for a pubic hair here but not there, but in *Counterpart*, one world interferes in the politics of the other world, and symmetry is lost with horrific consequences. Horrific consequences are the type of consequences often necessary for television series, although not perhaps for quantum mechanics in which mirror worlds may be permanently shut off from original worlds, shadows we and they may never see, never see our shadow selves, never see that mirrored darling, nor that mirrored world version of the cat we love so much.

Amanda Lear removed all mirrors from wherever it is she lives, Paris or somewhere steep and sunlit in Provence, or both, though I suppose London is not out of the question. Everywhere Amanda Lear lives she has removed every mirror, which seems out of character for the Amanda Lear character until it becomes clear that she has replaced all the mirrors in her homes with video cameras and screens which she uses to freeze-frame herself, facctune herself, edit her images, and stop herself looking anything other than exactly how she wants herself to look. In this way, for Amanda Lear, Amanda Lear's O-face and her M-face are no longer asymmetrical, but the rest of us might ask, which Amanda Lear is the mirror Amanda Lear, and do you even know who Amanda Lear is?

Worthy of the Event

My own mirror is the infinite space within which I prepare myself for here. My mirror is a shining world without Jacques Lacan and without constraints. In my mirror-world I am free to form myself as Body am I entirely, and nothing more. My M-world is a kind of factory version of the pool upon whose mirrored surface Narcissus caught a glimpse of himself and fell so entranced into the vision of his own beautiful being he forgot to do his hair, pluck his eyebrows, deal with those cuticles, do his nails, forgot to moisturize, and his serums sat unused forever, nor did he eat or sleep. Narcissus found himself in the mirror so hard and intense he stayed there with it until he died and U-Hauled off to the infinite.

✳

Full of visions that might seem hackneyed now but were not then, Antonin Artaud goes to Mexico in 1936, not specifically for teotl but in search of, he says, a sort of movement deep in Mexico in favour of a return to the civilization from before Cortez: The perfect example of primitive civilization with a spirit of magic [dot dot dot] healers and sorcercers on lost plateaux forests which speak and where the sorcerer with burnt fibres of Peyote and Marijuana still finds the terrible old man who teaches him the secrets of divination [dot dot dot] The basis of a magical culture which can `still gush forth the forces of the Indian earth` [dot dot dot] `the Mexicans of today dressed in the costumes of their ancestors, carrying out real sacrifice to the sun on the steps of Teotihuacan.`

It could be said that Antonin Artaud goes to Mexico as a way of crossing to another world beyond the world of his unhappy life in France, beyond the workings of his own mind, his disappointment with not-surreal-enough Surrealism, his poverty, and oh, the debts, but what he really goes for is in search of the bridge to another universe or to God.

He does not find any of it. He returns to Paris and predicts the end of dimensionality and reality as we know them and the arrival of a `Star which will occupy the entire surface of the air.` He is now thought to be lunatic, and he is forced into the psychiatric clinic of Ste. Anne where he has one session with Jacques Lacan who pronounces Artaud `chronically and incurably insane.`

`Lacan is an erotomaniac,` Antonin Artaud writes in one of his letters or notebooks, hitting the nail right on its head. In 1941, Robert Desnos, who is soon to die in the Theresienstadt concentration camp, has Antonin Artaud transferred to the asylum at Rodez, where it is warm and far enough, Robert Desnos hopes, from the German government of occupied France and its plans to cleanse France of Jews and lunatics, although, about this risk to himself, Antonin Artaud seems indifferent. He sees Adolf Hitler as a divine agent of the destruction necessary for the birth of a new world. At Rodez, Antonin Artaud undergoes *fifty-one* electro-convulsive therapy treatments, unmodified by muscle relaxants, and is put in a dozen or so insulin comas, both electric shock and insulin overdose intended to cure the sickness of his mind by inducing epileptoid seizures and silent coma. He draws more than he writes, and in Antonin Artaud's Rodez drawings, the body is often crucially doubled, just as life itself and theater itself are doubled in his earlier writings, as if Artaud is trying to show us a parallel or mirror world, another universe, or to show *himself*, but we do not see it, and even after the Germans have gone and Antonin Artaud is living comfortably in the garden pavilion at the Ivry-sur-Seine psychiatric clinic, hard at work, rectal cancer eating the rest of him, we still do not see what Antonin Artaud wants us to see, what Antonin Artaud wants Antonin Artaud to see, where he wants to be, and `Antonin Artaud starts screaming, his concern now is with infinity.`

※

My own concern now is about infinity and how to be worthy of it when it comes.

My question now is, did I go to Japan like Artaud went to Mexico in search of a past that never existed, a vanished world, hoping for a movement before or beyond my own time? Why Japan, people say to me much more often than they say, why woman, even though the two things entailed almost equal amounts of labor, equal commitments to the practice of love and learning to make me worthy. I went to woman because there was no other place to go. I went to Japan because there were so many other places to which I had already been. I went to Japan because a.k.a. Victor Mature had disappeared into something in Tokyo with an expense budget and he gave me a Japan Airlines ticket to Narita where it was snowing and dark and all the movement appeared to be toward the future until I realized, years it took, that every Japanese tree and stream, every waterfall and wave, every rock, every hill and mountain, every rice field and persimmon orchard, the air in all its seasons, the clouds and the skies, the sea itself teemed with gods and demiurges, swarmed with the essences of ancestors, with animalic ectoplasms, with hungry ghosts, shape-shifters, fox spirits, crane-wives, magical badgers, man-eating horses, Miyazawa Kenji, chrysanthemums in pots in Fall dispelling evil outside the houses, and after dark in the cities, fortune tellers appeared on some hyper-modern street corners.

I had to break a skin of ice to do my ablution at little Kawai-jinja, the shrine which sits not grand at all in the woods near the southern entrance to the grand Shimogamo shrine. Crack, crack, the ice said, and I said, oh see me waiting to go through, Tamayori-hime kamisama, who is a woman demiurge. I bought a wooden ema votive plaque done in the shape of a hand mirror. On one side of the wooden hand mirror were stencilled the basic lineaments of a human face. Next to the window where I bought the hand mirror ema there was a box of colored felt-tip pens. I took the red, black, green and brown and used them to turn the basic eyes and nose and mouth into beautiful complex

Worthy of the Event

eyes and a beautiful complex nose and a beautiful complex mouth, and on the other side of the wooden mirror I wrote, oh, kami-sama, make me beautiful enough to go through to the other side of the mirror forever, and then, with the snow circling down, I hung my wooden mirror with my submission on one side and my beautiful face on the other side among a million others asking for pretty much the same thing, except perhaps more heavily encoded:
```
Please find me a decent husband
I've bought the quince water
Please make my skin flawless
Stop my uncle
Take this fear from me
I can't live ugly
These pimples.
```
    Places like Kawai-jinja are portals to the sidereal, doorways opening onto completely abstracted ways of being. They are chutes through the mirror into other worlds and universes. They are places thick and gushing with flows of time past, time to come, time stilled forever. In places like Kawai-jinja haunts strew the alternate skies, astral beings hang in the air. Places like Kawai-jinja are infinity zones, yearning `to set afloat all those who are about to drown/in darkness whose depth they cannot know`. Places like Kawai-jinja dimple this whole world in which we live.

    All those times I hurled myself, hoping the tape would hold, from the golden cliff into the lagoon at Wattamolla, I was hoping the Dreaming could be for me *just this once* and the fish petroglyph on the rocks would swim up and catch me and bear me out to sea, forever. In the nave of Catedral de Sevilla I saw a door wide open into one of the Japanese hells, the hell called the Place of Filth, filled with steaming shit, excrescences of every kind, bitter and vile in your mouth; the hell where insects with hard stingers teem thick. In the Place of Filth, you are forced to eat the steaming shit, the oozing filth, infinitely, forever, crawling with fat white maggots. In the Place of Filth, the insects with hard stingers chew and pierce your skin; they gnaw your flesh and suck the marrow from your bones. I don't know why I saw one of the Japanese hells in an Andalusian cathedral but **run!** anyway.

Mandrake the horse stopped dead along the trail to Spider Rock and refused to move. When the light began to drain from the sky so high above the canyon rim and still Mandrake would not budge, Mr. Deschene said, "May as well set up camp now and don't you worry about what the horse knows is here."

Norma Mapagu says, "You are chronic. Your exoticizing is chronic. There will be consequences. Can't you find a way through to your own apotheosis in your own culture? Didn't you go to church a lot when you were a kid. Couldn't you see a way into heaven there?"

I say, "I wanted to live in The World, uppercase T, uppercase W, and living in The World is not the same as taking the world as your own, is it. Isn't living in The World why you moved here. To live in The World."

"Don't be a fool," Norma Mapagu says. "I traded myself to Stuart for a future for myself and my mother and father. All your blah blah blah blah blah blah about yearning for other worlds is just an excuse for your lifetime of cannabis,

Worthy of the Event

LSD, barbiturates, opiates, Polish vodka with grass in it, double Jack Daniel's on the rocks with a twist, I know, I do, shopping sprees, nihilism, and business class tickets you can't really afford, who cares about your inflammations, thank you, and what else, I don't know, *Buddhism*. Because you *could*. Unworthy, you can be."

That is really telling me.

Gertrude Stein's *Tender Buttons* is another reality within which English becomes other-dimensional:

```
A carafe, that is a blind glass

A kind in glass and a cousin, a spectacle
and nothing strange a single hurt color and
an arrangement in a system to pointing. All
this and not ordinary, not unordered in not
resembling. The difference is spreading.
```

※

As a child, Jeffrey Dahmer played games in which he consigned stick figure people to a black hole, that baffling symbol of all kinds of other-dimensionality, other-worldliness, and cosmic mystery. The event horizon was too much for the poor stick figures. They never returned. This Jeffery Dahmer story makes me worry about myself and my own yearning for other sides and for the alien infinite.

Might I be on the slippery slope to cannibalistic serial killer, I wonder. I do like to nip at my lovers, though not to make lunch of them and not in any throe of passion, but to test the meat of them before I go any further, and I *do* live in a world in which transsexual women can be depicted as grotesque predators, serial killers, *Psycho*, *Silence of the Lambs*, *Dressed to Kill*, all that talk about transsexual women sexually assaulting other women in women's lavatories and prison cells. It can be hard not to wonder about myself (demon?) although, while Jeffrey Dahmer consigned other people to the infinite, *I* want to consign *myself*, and not forever, if possible. I imagine returning with fabulously perplexing stories, a travel writer like no other, because seeing the infinite, seeing the eighth or fifth dimension, another universe, a mirror world, the far side of a black hole surely transforms everything you do from ordinary to astonishing.

By his own admission, until he saw the other side, Samuel Taylor Coleridge wrote only didactic poems, very *meh*. The doubled, mirrored, limitless worlds of "The Rime of the Ancient Mariner" and "Kubla Khan" seemed hidden to him until the milk of paradise, otherwise known as laudanum (alcohol spiked with raw opium), revealed both grandeur and horror in equal measure. In his notebook, Samuel Taylor Coleridge wrote:

```
a dusky light — a purple flash
crystalline splendour — light blue —
 Green lightnings —

in that eternal and delirious (misery)
 wrath fires —
 inward desolations
```

```
an horror of great darkness
great things — on the ocean
counterfeit infinity
```

Many of the men who painted miniatures to illuminate a manuscript or for collection in private muraqqa albums in fourteenth- to sixteenth-century Persia caught glimpses of other worlds and other dimensions after eating or drinking opium. If you look carefully at the backgrounds of some Persianate miniatures, you may discover hosts of uncanny faces and figures floating in the clouds or embedded in rocks. You may see skulls, a dragon, worm-like creatures watching the foreground of the painting where the main story occurs. `Only the beyond ultimately concerns us. The sense of a permanent power of transcendence over all limits — of openness to the infinite — is inseparable from the experience of consciousness,` says Roberto Mangabeira Unger, not so approvingly, but were Samuel Taylor Coleridge and the Persian miniaturists working at the opening between limit and limitless or just stoned out of their heads?

"Let's go and see those whirling dervishes," Fairy says.

Those Mevlevi Sufi in Konya spin themselves into the infinite. They whirl and turn in the sema, that dance and song *attributed* to Rumi. Around and around around around they go, pale skirts and tall hats, ecstasy just beneath the skin. Those Mevlevi Sufi pivot on the left foot, lift the right leg, put one hand up to heaven and one hand down to earth. Their heads do not move so that the syncope does not dizzy them. They do not fall down. They do not vomit like turning little girls in an Australian gloaming fall down and vomit. Those Mevlevi Sufi in Konya spin for an hour, and in that turning, they extinguish who they are here, and they bring to life who they are *there* in another dimension. Their tall black hats signify the tombstone, their black cloaks connote the tomb, and their flaring skirts mean the shroud, but those Mevlevi Sufi at Konya are not dying, they are life itself stretched across two dimensions, the mundane and the divine, this world and that world, and around they go, how they do turn, twirling off the lip of the planet, spinning beyond the limit of the circle, which is not set at the edge but at the utmost center where truth and purity barely move at all.

Watching those Mevlevi Sufi at Konya turning and turning and turning you cannot but want to turn and turn too and follow them to wherever it is they go, and if you have a spare couple of hundred US dollars, thirty-thousand yen, eighty Pounds Sterling, one hundred euro, you can learn dervish turning too. For a fee, you can spin until things seem better or at least different to here, for isn't that why so many human beings scan the far horizons, what we wonder about and long for now in the unending end of the world: a new dimension or another universe; a world much like this world, only disentangled from the past of our world; a world not on fire, not drowning, not riven by injustice and greed, not dancing to the song of more, *kaboom*, more, *ka-ching*, more, more; a *home* not subjected to the sight of nauseatingly wealthy men paying hundreds of millions of

Worthy of the Event

dollars to ride a rocket into near space as though their own excitement and the spectacle of priapic machines nuzzling up to the lips of the void might be enough to save us.

※

get out past the right-hand reef break
get out to deep
steer clear of Suicides
feel the kissing sun
fight the heavy barrel get out past abusive sea
past the local guys on their boards with that you-fucking-stupid-haole-chick look
not nasty, really, their hard white grins blowing away
on the soft trade winds
get out until a thick, smooth wave swells up maybe perfect as far as I know
and I catch it just right as far as I know
and that liquid surge I'm riding, now
riding in upon a fist
until I'm not, until the wave detonates
the board leash snaps
under I go, turning
sucked down
dragged out toward Mexico
rolled in toward the shore
crashedbangedscrapedscouredcorkscrewed
breathless across the sand and fangs of lava reef
spinning and bitten

lashed and flogged and
this is Just What I Want
give me the shock I want take me away make me the ocean I want
make me better make me different here in
sublime risk
sublime past art sublime and starry heavens sublime
all limits tested and crossed
Just What I Want extremity
the power of risk to bend the world and open the curve between here and there
my wave, my love, my wave sublime
my wave staggers. It coughs. My wave hawks me up onto the golden beach at Makapu'u where Teva Siu stands in the sun with my board in his hands, my body in his eyes. "That shore break here. You nearly lost it," he says, but I nearly *found* it, and that night we go to Kahala Beach and make out on the sand. Above, the heavens where Perseid meteors streak the sky with white fire. Teva Siu puts his lips upon my breast, so hard and round a planet might be in it. He whispers, "Nous sommes poussières d'étoiles." Those Tahitians, I think, and somewhere in another world, Krishna opens his mouth when Yashoda asks it of him. He has nothing to hide from his mother. She peers in, and there, beyond Krishna's cerulean lips, his little white teeth, and his shining pink tongue, she sees a garden, she sees endless universes, each with its own heaven and hell and every plane in between. Krishna's mother sees in her boy's mouth innumerable firmaments above continents, islands set in infinite oceans. In her son's mouth, Yashoda sees

storms, winds, toppling clouds and daggers of lightning, moons, planets, suns, and stars, black holes and coral reefs, vast nebulae and cosmic clouds, webs of energy. She sees everything probable and all possibilities and every hope and disappointment. She sees herself. "What am I seeing?" Yashoda wonders, "Can this be real?" and as soon as she thinks the question, she forgets what she has seen within Krishna's pretty little mouth, and she puts the child on her knee and tells him to stop eating dirt.

VII: the practice

When BamBam tells me he is not taking our relationship, which BamBam always calls *Us*, to the next level, I laugh. I laugh. I laugh, and when I laugh, BamBam takes my laugh poorly. It is not that BamBam does not long for the next level, he does, but BamBam does not want to want the next level. Nor is BamBam sure *I* want the next level. He balms his uncertainties by seeking to make me hurt about staying on this level or maybe even going to the basement where booty calls are kept. I know this and I will not let BamBam have it. So, I laugh. BamBam does not want me to laugh at him for not wanting the next level, so when I laugh laugh laugh, he shouts so loud half of Ramblewood can hear him. He shouts things like "You derivation. You cow in human form. You mutant. You bitch. You unoriginal imitation of a woman. Everything you fucking do and know is lifted. You owe me fifty. Go. Get out. Replicant," *etcetera*.

    I know all this is just BamBam's want-do-not-want-to-be-with-you-forever shit coming out, but he is correct: I *am* unoriginal. I *am* an awful imitator. I *emulate*, and not just to learn to drive a car con brio or cook a fish curry delicious or even to be a woman, although woman *did* require much downloading of selected forms, tropes, and tacit knowledges from the institutions of femininity long before downloading anything was a thing. Woman entailed a lot of picking up ways of being, especially how to open my legs and seem willing until, behold, I was able to become a me who also knew how to say no, nicely, and no, my copying ways, my imitations of life and thought and art and style and writing do not mean that I and my works are plagiarized. I do not do I do not do mimicry. I emulate.

•

Aemulatio

The Renaissance period brings the idea of aemulatio, expressing the challenge to creatively imitate famous examples instead of inventing new themes. Imitation was the basic rule, an attitude which covered most of the arts, finding expression in different ways: translatio (translate), imitatio (creative editing) or aemulatio (surpass). Every architectural example, classic or contemporary, could be copied as it was considered to be an honor when others emulated and varied one's work. In accomplishing this, an architect had to know the conventions (rules, regulations) of different architectural expressions, tools, and elements.

•

Emulation and imitation are the grounds upon which creation occurs. Practice is the method. Originality is an invention of the Industrial Revolution. It would take a book I do not have in me to show how nineteenth-century Euro-American ideas about creativity, inspiration, and originality are side effects of the factory. It would take another book to show how the split between emulation/imitation and creativity went from the ornate drawing rooms of Berlin and London into the discourses of colonialism, there to be used against local imitative and emulative practices to show how Japanese, Chinese, South Asians, Africans, and everybody other than white Europeans and Americans lacked creativity and originality and were mere copiers, and thereby, they and their works deserved contempt, deserved and required conquest and rectification to teach them how to be original. Imitation is, Charles Darwin's student George Romanes believed, intelligence of the second order and `even among idiots of a higher grade, of the 'feeble-minded,' a tendency to undue imitation is a very constant peculiarity. The same thing is conspicuously observable in the case of many savages.`

    I am savage. Doing how others have done before me is how *I* learn to do myself; it creates me; it fills me with skill and power. BamBam can say what he likes about copy. BamBam wants me to feel like a cheap copy of myself, but I am not a copy of anything. I am a perfect-perfectly-beautiful-even-in-my-flaws emulation of a perfect and perfectly beautiful way of being. The problem between me and BamBam is not me, it is BamBam in relation to me.

Worthy of the Event

The issue is what BamBam knows and feels when he lets my body into his story. I am stealth with BamBam, which means what stealth often means: I've not offered the whole story of my body and BamBam has not asked, although once in a room at the Fairmont Dallas and a heated argument about capital punishment, BamBam said, "You'd better get that bass out of your voice before your whole story falls apart."

So BamBam *knows*, but he knows in a way that doesn't want to know, except when he's lavishing his tongue and his lips and his fingers and his penis on those parts of my body made out of pills and surgeries and he gets too close, maybe, and my body makes him know his knowing. He comes too close to my body and too close to my body makes BamBam want to break it off and break away, dismantle the story we have together, this is not going to the next level, which is fine by me. I am not an elevator. I'm over the usual narrative forms, and, oh, go fuck yourself BamBam and no more bam-bambam-bam-bam-bam-bam-bam-bam bam-bambambam-bam-bam-bam-bam-bam bam-bam-bam-bam-bambam-bambam bam **bam** bam-bambambambam **bam aaaaaaa** and oh, baby, that's some gooooooooooooooooooooooood pussy.

※

I read Dodie Bellamy's "Barf Manifesto" and *then* I read Eileen Myles's "Everyday Barf." It was the wrong reading sequence, I know, going from what was inspired to the inspiration, from minor to major, from then to first, from the admiring essay to the essay so admired rather than the other way around, but, given both writers' wrecking ways with literary form, I suppose reading in reverse would not worry them much. Anyway, both essays have vomit on them. "Everyday Barf" is a tour de force of poem-transitioning-to-essay.

Eileen Myles pukes all over the everyday, messes up the quotidian, and around them on the fast boat from Provincetown people barf and throw up on the floor and each other, and Eileen Myles's essay sheds its form as they lean into the sounds of spewing, `wha whaa blah urp,` and they write a sestina for publication and write a poem to their mother and the words stream and slide off the page and Bob Dylan sits at the deathbed of Woody Guthrie, `urp.`

"Barf Manifesto" is Dodie Bellamy's response to "Everyday Barf." It is both homage to Eileen Myles and a writing practice emulating, or inspired by, the technique and the political principles driving Eileen Myles's technique. Dodie Bellamy says she began her aemulatio with an attempt to copy the structure and form of "Everyday Barf", but `I churned out adolescent garbage,` and she started again. Dodie Bellamy *does* vomit mimetically in the published version of "Barf Manifesto" and she *is* concerned with essay form in the same way that Eileen Myles is concerned with essay form, but "Barf Manifesto" is all Dodie Bellamy close reading and recruiting and recutting Eileen Myles's piece onto an expanded stage, refaceted so that barf now sheds light on both the personal and the political. Dodie Bellamy's aemulatio of "Everyday Barf" teaches Dodie Bellamy a great deal of what she needs to know to write "Barf Manifesto."

※

By the time I got to the Eileen Myles and Dodie Bellamy essays and the want to emulate them came up, I'd been emulating writers almost forever. I taught myself how *not* to do what Dylan Thomas did by stealing *Collected Poems* from right under the nose of Miss Fields, Librarian, bearing it home furtive and dry with guilt, and cutting a dozen poems into single words and rearranging the cut-ups into new poems which tried, but quite failed, fortunately, to emulate Dylan Thomas's meter and rhythm. I had pangs about what I did with poor *Eunuch Dreams*, and you know why. Also, I once copied *Mrs Dalloway* into every second line of a dozen lined exercise books and then tried to emulate what Virginia Woolf does with narrative voice, structure, cadence, and syntax to write a novelette about a woman in a fishing village in Australia on the blank lines. This took two years and was a secret and I only managed ten thousand words. You may also find in me emulations of Gertrude Stein's punctuation. My foolhardy relationship with the paratactic conjunction – blah blah, and blah blah and blah blah and blah blah and blah blah and so on until you can no longer sustain it and run out of ands – and my slavish idolization of the sentence with ten thousand parts to it are results of many practices on Johann Peter Hebel's ways with lots and lots of "and", and many experiments with long-haul sentences in the prolix style of W. G. Sebald's *Vertigo* and *The Rings of Saturn*. Hilary Mantel's profligate habits with the semicolon are here right now; I have *practiced* her, and if such practices have mimetic qualities, always of style and form rather than the thing itself, that does not result in copies or mimicry but in a kind of *representation* of the emulated text, which might itself be a dead end except for Walter Benjamin's view that the so-called dead end of representation is, in fact, that dangerous moment at which an entirely new way of writing the world may appear.

※

The first thing to make me want to emulate "Everyday Barf" and "Barf Manifesto" was Eileen Myles's mention of political sestina. Not that I can write poetry, but I *do* read poetry for what it teaches me about precision with language. To be honest, I am less well-read than I pretend to be, and sestina was new to me, and new-to-me is a condition that makes me compulsive in a good way, compulsive enough to look sestina up and read about sestina and think about writing a sestina in response to "Everyday Barf", except I am not good at numbers and I am also in a kind of long-term recovery from a pathological fear of rules and too much obedience, so, after texting Norma Mapagu about it, I decided that writing a sestina would be too far and too hard and would teach me a lot I already knew about knuckling under but nothing about writing in the way that Eileen Myles and Dodie Bellamy write.

The second thing that made me want to practice essay with "Everyday Barf" and "Barf Manifesto" was stuff coming out of bodies. How I like that, *emissions*. I could do that. I have several decent vomit stories: how Norma Mapagu once wrote a vomit sonnet; how a.k.a. Victor Mature drank too many Harvey Wallbangers under the chandeliers at a cocktail party thrown by Rupert Murdoch at the original Waldorf Astoria, and how a.k.a. Victor Mature then puked convulsively in the cab taking him back to the original Plaza Hotel and caught the barf in his hands and stuffed it into the pockets of his antelope-suede jacket and acted in the cab and with the doorman at the original Plaza like nothing had happened, nothing smelled like canapes and Harvey Wallbanger barf; how Grandpa Dilt took my mother and me way out on the glaucous morning sea in a dinghy and I vomited white toast and pink quince jam and a boiled hen's egg onto the steely and barely heaving water and a little school of silvery flathead or bream or mullet came to the surface like left-over shards of moonlight and ate my barf, and Grandpa Dilt scooped them up with a net and bits of half-digested toast and egg and my mother said, "Dinner"; how a man sitting across the aisle from me on an old Air Lanka Boeing 707, on heaving final approach to Colombo at night, barfed and tried to hold his barf in with his hands clamped over his mouth but the puke spurted between his fingers so hugely accelerated by the force required to escape through the very narrow spaces between his phalanges, so powerful, his barf sprayed all of us in rows 34 to 28 with what had recently been, south of Great Andaman, a nice mackerel curry and white rice and then we landed; how once I was giving Harry head and too deep throat too soon after dinner, `urp`.

"Derivation and emulation are not the same thing. Reconsider barf as a topic," Norma Mapagu says on Messenger when I message her about my vomit stories. She always knows.

Dodie Bellamy knows too; she knows better than to do more than a quick vomit à la Myles in "Barf Manifesto" but she does keep the bodily emissions thing going with a bit of a shit story about Eileen Myles not having toilet paper in their house and shitting in Eileen Myles's toilet and using paper kitchen towels to wipe her ass and the paper towels block Eileen Myles's funky old pipes and mortify, even anger, Dodie Bellamy, who keeps trying to stuff her floating shit down the S-bend and feels ill-used by Eileen Myles for it all.

"What about shitting," I DM Norma Mapagu, still on Messenger. "Nobody writes about shitting. Where's the shitting in *The Charterhouse of Parma*? Who does the shitting in Proust? Who takes out the shit in *Slouching Toward Bethlehem*?"

Norma Mapagu texts: "Also, shitting has yet to win the Booker Prize. Think about that. Prepare for rejection."

I *do* think about that, a lot, rejection, not because of the Booker Prize, which is no closer than Alpha Centauri for me, but because I am not good with rejection – it feels like there has been a *lot* of it – and so, I am ready to give up shitting, if I can, because one more no: who needs it? But if not shitting, what emission for the practice? Maybe snot or pus or even jism of any sort, although any snot worth writing about is the sort of snot that kills the snotter unless you suck it out with a machine. Pus is, well: even though my sister and I found bursting boils and carbuncles delightful and fulfilling until we were about twelve and the arrival of pimples and do *not*, not, never ever squeeze, pus is even more pathological than snot; I don't mind putting readers off, making them go yuck, erk, gross, how *revolting*, we are really uncomfortable now, but I don't want to put readers off so much they toss the book aside and watch YouTube Shorts about BB crème or Emirates business class instead. Also, not everybody gets pussy (or is it pussey?), not everybody has had pus, not everybody has experienced the pus of others even at a bit of a distance. Maybe an essay about body emissions needs to be an essay about the unavoidable, everybody-everybody-has-dealt-with-it kinds of emission, and pus is not that, is it? Sexual emissions have no story beyond somebody did something right, and really, swallowing and/or smearing jism on your face are mostly just things you do because swallowing and smearing make you look good.

Q: Why do I not consider urine?

A: I have bad memories of yellow.

"Growths, even *warts*," I say to Norma Mapagu.

"Just go back to your usual themes, why not, to beauty, or what about wonder, awe, courage, some transcendence is always good," she says.

Shit can transcend, can't it? What about the shit passages in Ito Hiromi's *Togenuki Jizo: Shin Sugamo Jizo engi*, which has been translated into English and called *The Thorn Puller*? Ito Hiromi is not shy of shit; she has no problem publishing her shit; her shit rises above itself. Ito Hiromi's shit wins literary prizes. Read the scenes in which the narrator attends to her mother's efforts to shit, yotto yotto, the mother is trying very hard, yotto yotto, to shit, until at last, Mom said, oh, it feels like something's coming. A soft, slippery bowel movement slid out, and I wiped her clean. I said, Mom, come forward a little bit, and she swayed her body as she leaned forward. Yotto. As a young mother, I'd done the same thing countless times. My baby's bottom was smooth and pale pink. What came out was yellow and green and so pretty I could almost imagine mistaking it for pudding and giving it a taste. It smelled slightly sour like spoiled milk, so it seemed a gross exaggeration to label it "shit." That's why I started using the cuter, more benign-sounding "poop." Compared to those baby bowel movements, Mom's loose stools were shit. They had the same foul smell as the ones I make. Each time she used the toilet, I had to stick my hand in and help her wash. It wasn't long before my hand started to smell.

Worthy of the Event

Now I am back to shit in a big way. Ito Hiromi's shit convinces me I can do a practice with shit on Eileen Myles and Dodie Bellamy. And anyway, shit is natural to me. I am like a fly about shit. I can rise above my own shit. I am *on* it. I've *always* looked in the bowl after and I've often thought about how shit and shitting are heavily euphemized and technically unmentionable among human beings, except within the family, and even then, some families don't, and yet, everybody talks about shit and shitting if they can, especially in their silences about shit, they talk. The unmentionable is highly discursive, never more so than when the institutions of the state try to keep shit out of sight and out of language, for example, that shit situation at the historic settler village of Richmond in Tasmania where there is a museum of shit and the local government spent three years trying to remove a sign showing a penguin doing projectile shit and trying to remove a small bronze of a dog taking a shit outside the Pooseum where `talking about poo is not taboo.` It is all too big and has the wrong *orientation* for the historic character of Richmond, the mayor is said to have said, making the topic of shit *appear* when he intended *disappear*.

※

Eileen Myles likens the opened boot or trunk lid of their car to a completely open ass- or arse-hole, and here I am. Look, I am clearing shit out of my house, `dollops of it`, and I am loading the cleared-out shit into the open behind of the black Volvo and then driving all this shit to the local drop-off spot for shit. There is a good view of the shit-colored river there, and I am pulling this old shit out of the arse/ass of the black Volvo trunk/boot like I once pulled stalled, impacted shit from the rectum of Mr. Arthur, who was seventy-three years of age and who had not had a bowel movement beyond a dark and cruelly ironic pebble every three days for two months and the aperients only blowing up thunderous storms of gas. "Attempt manual removal, Nurse," Charge-Nurse Vinogradoff commanded in the way which had seen her through, or was developed in, I don't know, deportation from Minsk to a Third Reich labor unit in Norway, a displaced persons camp near Hamburg, a voyage via Dakar, Cape Town, and Colombo to Australia, a year in a refugee camp, learning how to be a *New* Australian and forever grateful for the chance, aren't you, not easy, that, and there was I, another kind of refugee, learning to be a nurse as a way of escaping striptease and lip-syncing Lainie Kazan and sucking dicks for twenty dollars a pop no kissing, hoping for a future to make something of yourself, not easy, that. There was I, double-gloved and masked and as close to elbow-length fisting as I would ever get, pulling lumps out of a man's rectum and dropping them into a commode, and Mr. Arthur said, "Thanks, thank you, Nurse, I feel better already," and he eyed the little cairn of his accumulated ejecta as if saying goodbye and he closed his eyes and smiled. He was, at last, unplugged, oh, the relief of it, and for the next three minutes Mr. Arthur emitted an avalanche of cack ploploploploploploploploploploploploplop and he said, "Oh, yairs, that feels really good," and his eyes rolled up into his head searching for something in his brain and Mr.

Worthy of the Event

Arthur sighed, he sagged, he slumped, and Charge-Nurse Vinogradoff came at a clip and felt Mr. Arthur's pulse, and said, "It seems, Nurse, you've killed him," and Mr. Arthur was *dead* just like that, in a millisecond, as if all that had kept him alive was the feculent train of shit in his gut holding him together like a spine or an intention or a belief or a *relationship*. Mr. Arthur's content had gone, and without it he was nothing but form. Charge-Nurse Vinogradoff said, I must say, Mr. Arthur did his death in a worthy of it sort of way.

※

Until I read "Everyday Barf" and "Barf Manifesto", I'd not given much (any) thought to the matter of literary form and literary content. I had not thought at all about what Eileen Myles says is the `real honest engagement` literary form has with literary content, and even after finishing this emulative writing practice with both essays, I still don't know much, I still don't know if form controls content or content controls form or if it's some dialectical honest relationship going on between them. To be honest, I doubt I've had an honest relationship in my entire life, and honest engagements, well, give me a diamond ring or something bling (not tiara), as three have, indeed, done. And anyway, doesn't Morris Weitz think, and vehemently, that the distinction between form and content is not only uninformative, but actively misleading, `responsible for more of the difficulties` in contemporary aesthetic thought than any other, not to mention *not interesting*, even though *not interesting* is a hard thing to say in connection with Eileen Myles anything, although I don't know how interesting they would be as a guest at a dinner party on the lanai and that Prussian-blue view of the gloaming sea. Writers are often not.

Dismantlement is what happens to the essay form, Dodie Bellamy reckons, when the human body is the essay content. She can take that view because she's got some French going on in her writer's head. She's got the dregs of Georges Bataille swaggering about in her veins. She's got a soupçon of Georges Bataille's view that the erotic body in the text demolishes conventional literary ways with form and content, wreaks une dissolution des formes constituées, although by the time of "Barf Manifesto", Dodie Bellamy has exceeded her Bataille and become a bit post-erotic-post-Bataille post-*Cunt-ups* and post-getting-fucked-upside-down-under-bad-lighting in *the buddhist*. In "Barf Manifesto" Dodie Bellamy's French has gone somehow from Georges Bataille to a bit Julia Kristeva. She's gone from Vézelay to Île de Ré. She's gone from Georges Bataille's erotic body to Julia Kristeva's bodily emissions which have the power to *nauseate* and demolish the essay's usual forward propulsion of the narrative arc, that fantasy of progress, resolution.

✳

Worthy of the Event

Well, Mr. Arthur's shitting body certainly demolishes Mr. Arthur's narrative arc, for him and for me, that is for sure. The shit stops the fantasy of progress and Mr. Arthur's story ends before the end for me, he departs this practice, dismantles the story and leaves me with where the practice essay is now to go.

Where to go: I could unreel nurse stories at this point. I could take advantage of the good transition available from Mr. Arthur's inadvertent death-by-nurse in hospital to more nurse stories, for nurse stories have a history of yearning to be told, beginning with the story of Florence Nightingale and her lamp and those poor soldiers maimed and dismembered by Russian guns at Crimea while rich tourists from London and Birmingham picnicked in the sunshine with a view of the blue Black Sea and a beautiful panorama of soldiers falling. And some people *do* say to me, "You should write about that nursing you were, the asylum, the hospital," but even though nurse stories are often formed out of a relationship with bodies, they are not *of* the body itself, and how much `dissolution des formes constituées`, how much demolition of the essay form, how *nauseating* could a nurse story be, always canting toward the clean and tidy as nurse stories do, always leaning organized, ridden by the law as nurse stories are, like the duties of nurses and nurses themselves, and seemingly invulnerable, nurses, aren't they, even during COVID-19 and millions of bodies, the form and content of the nurse story held together. Never underestimate Nurse.

✵

Never underestimate shit. We are born in it. Maggie Nelson knows that: `Then they say I can push. I push. I feel him come out, all of him, all at once. I also feel the shit that had been bedeviling me all through pregnancy and labor come out too. My first feeling is that I could run a thousand miles, I feel amazing, total and complete relief, like everything that was wrong is now right.` And often we die with a shit: a little squirt when the bullet pierces the frontal lobes; a whole dump when the hangman's noose strangles the shit out of you; or you shit as things shut down and you cannot help it, maybe don't even know it, sometime in those final hours when peristalsis clears the way for death. To Nurse, and to your friends and family, if they are there when that final dump is taken, that last shit signifies departure from the social aspects of human being, for to open your bowels willy-nilly is a disgrace after the age of three or four or even earlier, and a sign of something seriously wrong in adults. We are disgusted by and ashamed of our own shit. We hide it and recoil at the shit of others because shit holds the secret of us: we are not angels.

✵

Email with attachment to Norma Mapagu: "Read this, would you. I'm trying to emulate Dodie Bellamy's voice, so cool and detached even when her form and content relationship gets hot and crazy."

Worthy of the Event

Think big about shit. Each pile of shit is a kind of civilization itself, chock-a-block with microscopic and sub-microscopic beings, more than a trillion living and other organisms in every gram of crap. Shit in one form or another is a planet within the planet of every living body and within the body of Planet Earth, all overpopulated, reeking, fighting for survival or, at least, stability, and all heading for the flush button and existential transubstantiation from autonomous and special subject to just another excreting organism, human being, spotted dog, bristly pig, chestnut horse, singing whale, angelfish like precious jewel, tardigrade, honey bee, jellyfish, emu. Shit shapes who we are and how we can be in the world. Metabolic syndromes, chronic inflammatory diseases, sickening anxiety, and the kind of depression that seems without cause are all connected to shit and ask any person with celiac disease or ulcerative colitis or a colostomy bag about what happens to work, fun, romance, sex, food, and who you think you are when conditions on your own shit planet go awry. If the gut is the second brain, then shit is the ideas this brain produces and puts out in the world. Ask yourself how many policies, both good and bad, have been formed by constipation, by its opposite, or by nice, regular bowel movements, and what about the bowel habits that may have started and ended wars: John F. Kennedy had chronic diarrhea; Adolf Hitler suffered from bouts of diarrhea so debilitating he took opiates to relieve the symptoms and then it was impossible to shit and you know how bitter and twisted that makes you.

Email to me from Norma Mapagu: "Oh, stop it. Just use your normal STYLE, which I miss. You may take that as a compliment."

Email with attachment to Norma Mapagu:
Late-stage-I-hope capitalism is founded upon a planetary kingdom of ten thousand shit-related things and systems and discourses: billions of shit receptacles, of which the Toto Washlet smart toilet is Queen; a special throne room for shitting, one for guests and one for each bedroom if there is money or credit at the bank; pipes and sewers and drains and outfalls and sewage treatment plants and whole forests made into paper for wiping shitty cracks; soap and disinfectants and air fresheners, diapers, a grand bazaar of poo-related medicaments, and the moral economy of hygiene and privacy, wash your hands, don't

play with your shit, don't play with your arsehole, don't be an asshole, clean the bowl, flush, do not shit here, watching you shit does not give me an erection, oh, yuck. Is it any wonder that losing his shit killed Mr. Arthur? "Oh dear, but he looks pleased!" Charge-Nurse Vinogradoff said, "Everything wrong is right for him now, I suppose," and thereby, Mr. Arthur returns to this emulation, this writing practice. His dear old, vulnerable body sits up for two more lines; he might want to stay, he might yearn to be an integrating device, but I will not not let Mr. Arthur come back for more because I killed him and because demolished essay does not mean chaotic essay, and shit is the integrating thing, and repetition of Maggie Nelson's everything that was wrong is now right, not Mr. Arthur, is the tool to keep demolition from dropping bricks on readers' heads. This is the practice.

"Is that better?"

※

Miss Elaine Tutty, Miss we-never-knew-your-given-name-but-the-rumor-is-Celeste Bond, Miss Beverly Rye, and Miss Valmae Heggy. These four women taught me to write English and to play the alto recorder, although not at the same time. Miss Tutty was large, she was pink, she was *emotional* with her ruler or with my ruler, whichever came to hand. Miss we-never-knew-your-given-name-but-the-rumor-is-Celeste Bond was small and brittle and had red hair in that rare Titian shade of red hair, no freckles, and she arrived at us seared and relieved and bitter after three years out there at a school in Meekatharra. Miss Rye had ways with corporal punishment needful of no implement. Miss Heggy: upslanted eyes and nervous skin. The method of the Misses Tutty Bond Rye Heggy with me was invariable. It was all copy practice copy hit or threaten to hit practice copy practice copy practice hit or threaten to hit copy practice hit emulate practice hit emulate practice or threaten to hit, hit practice practice practice practice. I got used to it. I was used to hit and the threat to hit from elsewhere.

Who cared?

I liked copy.

I liked emulation.

I liked practice. Practice was all form and no content unless I thought of the words with meaning I could make with those twenty-six beautifully cursive letters; unless the lyrics to "Londonderry Air" occurred to me as I played the first bars of the second verse: `But come ye back when summer's in the meadow`. There was pleasure in practice. I liked looking at the examples of perfect upper-case As and perfectly formed curly lower-case Esses and trying over and over again to copy them. I like writing the same letter to Grandma over and over again. I liked looking at some étude in "Music for a While Adapted for the Alto Recorder" and playing the first eight bars ten thousand times until Miss Beverly Rye told me I could go on to the next eight bars. I liked repetition. Again, and again, and again had its rewards, and not just the intangible reward of a kind of stillness within which skills accrued. Not even the reward of emulation well done. Again-and-again-and-again materialized me and gave me my body.

All that copy practice emulate practice repeat with the alto recorder got me a prize for best solo recorder performance at the local eisteddfod. All that copy practice emulate practice repeat with cursive writing and the epistolary form also got me writing letters full of lies and not about my life to one grandmother, a great-aunt, and a pen pal in Lansing, Michigan. Great-Aunt Clarice Willoughby rewarded a well-written letter with a ten-shilling note or, after decimalization, a one-dollar note, by mail. When ten shillings did not come despite three letters about, one, a UFO landing on the hills we all called Bosoms Hills, then snickered; two, how Him had taught me to drive his new green car; and three, watching *Swan Lake* on television for the first time at Second-Cousin-Once-Removed Aileen's house in Panania (this, at least, was true), I borrowed Franz Kafka's *Letters to Milena* from the Wagga Wagga Public Library. "Let her have what she wants," my mother said to the raised librarian eyebrows of Miss Rhonda Duffy, although my mother used a different pronoun, and I read Franz Kafka's letters and then tried to emulate his epistolary form and content in my next letter to Great-Aunt Clarice Willoughby. Success. Ten shillings.

I did it again with Kafka. One dollar. And again, this time practicing letter writing with Rainer Maria Rilke's *Letters to a Young Poet*, at which point, Great-Aunt Clarice sent a card with a reproduction of an Albert Namatjira watercolor of the vermilion and lilac country around Alice Springs on it and inside: `I cannot afford you. Keep practicing but stop copying. Find pleasure in being creative, that is my advice to you.`

※

Elizabeth Anscombe thought human beings *always* provide a reason for failure but not often for pleasure. Elizabeth Anscombe was like *that* with Ludwig Wittgenstein, I have read. She was edgy, admired for her philosophical works, and a bit notorious for raising seven children, chain-smoking cigars, and wearing pants to an audience with the Pope, a fashion choice that might be shock-horror even now. There might be shock-horror about Elizabeth Anscombe's enthusiastic Catholicism, which, one tends to forget, is still, in a way, a *dissident* position in the United Kingdom. Elizabeth Anscombe might be criticized for her criticism of contraception and for her opposition to men having sex with men, which she presented in the form of a sophisticated philosophical exegesis upon how Roman Catholic natural law requires submission to a minimum of three propositions: first, there are some universal and immutable *moral* truths; second, human beings have the capacity to know these *moral* truths; third, human nature is the basis on which these *moral* truths are known. It's hard not to laugh. Elizabeth Anscombe pronounced *shitting* as *shit-ting*, the two t's sounded separately like one of those Japanese doubled consonants, Nip-pon: `Many of my friends tell me that they take great pleasure in shit-ting. I myself do not choose to pursue this pleasure. But I do not feel that I need an excuse` (hyphen added), she said in some lecture, but is Elizabeth Anscombe saying that she does not shit, she does not shit *intentionally*, her shit-ting is not pleasurable, or that she is ascetic about it, or that she does shit and it does feel good but she doesn't pursue the causes of why shit-ting feels so good.

※

Many people take pleasure in doing the traditional essay form. I have been one of them. I have taken. Mastery of the rules has its satisfactions. Dodie Bellamy is not one of those people. She is anhedonic about the traditional essay form. She still does it for the money, but she takes no pleasure by it, she longs to be free of it, she longs for the pleasure to be had from throwing the body and its emissions at the usual essay and watching the essay collapse into innovative but still-meaningful rubble. I want Dodie Bellamy's pleasure for myself. *That* is the practice. "You will never get a piece about shit published," Norma Mapagu says again, and it turns out Norma Mapagu knows what she is talking about.

I could throw my own body at the essay form. I could throw the bodies of others and see what comes down. I could throw the neovagina into content. I could test the demolition powers of the sex-changed transsexual body against `forward propulsion of the narrative arc, that fantasy of progress, resolution`. I mean, neovagina troubles a lot of systems, and changing your sex, changing a sex/gender embodiment, disrupts the even surfaces of many social and political forms, demolishes the law and good manners equally, turns wise speech into falling bricks of violent rhetoric, words into fists on bodies. Surely, the dick-and-tits Venn diagram thing or the neovagina speaking from my own body or from Big Denise's body would make short work of the usual essay form. But then, and don't mention this "but then" to Norma Mapagu, who might only like me because she sees my body as somehow revolutionary even though she's never actually seen my body; but then, there is the matter of essays written by a transsexual woman *about* transsexual bodies: no demolition of the essay form happens there, believe me. And then there is the matter of transsexual-woman memoir which, with only a couple of exceptions (in English), cleaves to and grips the `forward propulsion of the narrative arc, that fantasy of progress, resolution` as though terrified of drowning in a formless sea: troubled child, realization that there is female inside the male body, a bad case of gender dysphoria, much suffering, coming out, gender transition, oh joy!, more suffering, then some sort of détente. All that lovely old transsexual shit.

Worthy of the Event

✷

Old white capri pants, turned to shit now my butt has gone big, come from the open ass of my car, and there is a stain, much bleached and scrubbed and OxiCleaned and sunned to a barely perceptible straw color, but still looking like a shit stain from Istanbul in 2007 when the white capri pants are new and perfect for the summer day, but also when I have previously eaten too much köfte from beneath the warming lights at that büfe we couldn't go past, and now I have to get to a toilet, oh, very quick. I rush home, tumble down the dizzying jagged steps of Çihangir with a view of a Russian freighter going up the Bosporus in the sunshine, Fairy behind me, and just as I get up the terrazzo stairs that always smell of cat pee to the front door on the fourth-floor landing, and just as I reach for the key, I relax just a bit too soon and Fairy says behind me, "Your shit is making an appearance on your bottom. It looks like a brown triangle. It is the shape of a Tasmania. Are there koalas in it."

I can't laugh without putting the lot in my white capri pants. I say, "There are no koalas in Tasmania, and have you ever seen a triangular turd." The door is open now, oh, quickquick.

"I never look at my own," Fairy says, untruthfully, and I have evidence. "But I saw on my handy that wombat poo comes out in cubes."

Fairy has a sore throat again. When she talks, she sounds like Marlene Dietrich, and even though I am about to shit myself, lust comes up surprising, but hardly surprising.

Libido and toilet are not strangers. Fairy and I sometimes pee on each other in the shower although with *a lot* of liquid soap, she is always hygienic, and "Plop, plop, schatz," Fairy says and makes a kissing sound with those black-cherry lips, and I am ploploploploploploploploploploplop.

My almost-disaster with my own shit in Istanbul makes Fairy feel better about herself. She loves a moment of schadenfreude, who does not, even the Buddha himself must have had a moment of pleasure at the sight of his Self scuttling away to oblivion, tears in its eyes. Fairy hates everything that comes out of her own body, especially shit, which Fairy might think exposes something intrinsically rotten about her; we never talk about it, so I don't know for sure, I am inferring, but this is what I *see*: When Fairy needs to poo, she has to lock the toilet door and check the lock several times. She has to wait until she's washed her hands and cleaned her teeth and lined the toilet seat even in her own home with thirteen layers of toilet paper, and she must stuff more paper in the cracks around the door and start the water running or start A-ha or Take That on her phone, by which time the shit has gone back up so she has to sit on the papered seat and wait for it to come down again, and once it's all out and swept around the S-bend or whatever letter of the alphabet accords with the shape of the plumbing, Fairy has to spray the room with something citrus only and wash her hands and clean her teeth and sniff the air for taint and dispose of all the extra toilet paper used on the seat and in the gaps around the door and finally Fairy comes out as the woman who never has a bowel movement. She returns to me as a body without organs. She is reorganized. She is a virtual person now but destined for actuality and IRL again when her bowels reappear or when I put my tongue on her in a certain way or when there is cake or sausage present.

✳

Cow in Gertrude Stein seems to be sometimes a word for orgasm and sometimes a word for shit: And now a little scene with a queen contented by the cow which has come and been sent and been seen. A dear dearest queen. My sweet dear does hear her dear here saying little and big coming and true discern and firmly coming out softly shoving out singly coming out all of the cow that has been registered as a round now. Navigation submarine of the cow come out of queen my queen. That is what the cow does it sinks and a little it sinks so sweetly, my own cow out of my queen own is now seen.

Gertrude Stein's work on Alice B. Toklas's cows demolishes something, but what? Does demolition of the line between coming cow and shitting cow tear things down or is it Gertrude Stein's demolition of sentence structure and narrative trajectory that destroys the edifice? Gertrude Stein almost always writes in this form, no matter the content, and Alice B. Toklas's cows, *plop plop* or *oh, darling*, are very much under Gertrude Stein's control.

✳

Harry sends me a pile. Harry sends more than one hundred and fifty-three English language synonyms and collocations for shit and shitting. Harry says better not forget that story about a man in the bar at the Hong Kong Sheraton who offered to pay my room bill and give me ten thousand Hong Kong dollars if I squatted and shat on the glass coffee table in his suite while he jerked off underneath looking up at my shitting ass. And Harry wants me to include the story of Maria M., who is known now mostly by her deadname because Maria M.'s life and who she was have been demolished by mostly gay male not-trans-anything academics who, in their quests for tenure and for grants to fund summers in Italy and for transgressive heroes for *themselves*, dismantle, shatter, and *de-transition* Maria M. post-mortem; they turn her into he, they redact the transsexual woman right out of her, turn Maria M. into themselves, and never mention what Maria M. said about herself: I believe that my erotic desire for women is deeply alive in me, it is deeply located in my desire to be woman. But if you look at photographs of Maria M., you see she's as trans as transsexual is, she is as travesti as travesti could be in Italy in the 1970s, oh, those sunglasses and that femme embodiment.

Maria M. ate shit on stage in *La traviata norma, ovvero: Vaffanculo... ebbene sí*. Post-prandial, she invited the audience to fuck her ass because she wanted to show the alchemical power shit has to conquer the Real, to unbind the

Worthy of the Event

"straight-fuck-binomial-gender-prison-capitalist-class-structure-hell" containing us all. Maria M. thought coprophagy and a form of anality that is way beyond men-who-have-sex-with-men anality, and way beyond straight ass-fucking, would conjure an otherwise. Eating shit would disrupt the Levitical division of clean and dirty and release another way of being, which, as far as Maria M. was concerned, was transsexuality, although not the transsexuality of gender clinics and self-help forums and social justice, but a transsexuality that is a revolutionary consciousness *and* the primal condition of all human beings until the child is flayed into male or female. Maria M.'s revolutionary pleasure of shit exceeded coprophilia and ass fucking shit pleasure; it overtook even the pleasure of shit-ting described by Elizabeth Anscombe. Maria M.'s shit pleasure was jouissance, the pleasure of rights and appropriation of property, the pleasure of fighting back, the pleasure of orgasm and touch, the pleasure of choosing shit in your mouth, oh, how much I admire Maria M., but eating shit would be taking this practice too far, and barf. Urp.

I am not saying Maria M. was original in her shit-eating performance. There was a lot of shit-eating in the nineteen-seventies. There was Divine eating fresh dog shit in *Pink Flamingos*. There was the shit-eating scene in *Gravity's Rainbow*: The turd slides into his mouth, down to his gullet. He gags, but bravely clamps his teeth shut.

Spasms in his throat continue. The pain is terrible. With his tongue he mashes shit

```
against the roof of his mouth and begins
to chew, thickly now, the only sound in
the room.
```
    For all I know, Maria M. might have been emulating, even copying John Waters and Thomas Pynchon; she might have been emulating an older shit-eating story by the Marquis de Sade in which a man asks his wife to suck him off while she shits in his mouth. I am pretty sure Maria M. and John Waters and Thomas Pynchon and the Marquis de Sade understood the power of shit itself and the power of shit in the mouth especially to upset everything about how things are supposed to be and be done.

※

I spend one year and two months translating the poems of Kaneko Mitsuharu, who never copied nor imitated anything that I know of. "He is an individualist," O says. She would know.
    When I read the poems of Kaneko Mitsuharu, I don't know what I'm reading except to know that beautiful Japanese poetry cannot be said of Kaneko Mitsuharu poems. He does not much bother with the winged line of a temple roof, the morning bell, the withering of a spring blossom, the full moon gelid in the evening sky, the largo plonk of a bamboo sōzu in some garden, the charms of impermanence.
    Before beginning, I imagine my translation work to be a form of copying Japanese poetry into English. In the doing, though, my translation work turns out to be a kind of

literary emulation barely tethered to the original form and content, almost floating off by itself, more like writing a new poem than transferring an existing poem into another language. Kaneko Mitsuharu's political poems have lots of declarations in them. In Japanese, the declarations are not beautiful, no, but they have some untranslatable lyrical economy to them which turns out to be impossible for me to imitate or even emulate in translation. No matter how much my translations massage them, Kaneko Mitsuharu's declarations come out all blunt and all political pamphlet. I work the poems so hard they become my own poems, and I am not a poet. My translations end up so far from the Japanese poems, I hate what I have done, I hate myself for not being able to emulate art, and I hate Kaneko Mitsuharu and all his works, for years, I really hate him and his poems but then I get to his ero jiisan horny, romantic old-man poems, especially one poem:

<u>another poem</u>

```
my darling.
finally I've turned
into your shit
the larvae of flies
tickle me
and all the other shits
down in the little shitcan
not one bitter smidgen in me darling
to be digested
down to dregs
```

```
and pushed out by you
floating up sinking down
calling to you, my darling
yet no way you hear me
the one turned to shit
the toilet door squeaks and you're out
 with a bang
```

and suddenly I love Kaneko Mitsuharu and his poems.
  "Love is shit," says Big Denise.

✵

Almost every year there is some scandal about some writer emulating other writers too much. I have read that T.S. Eliot over-emulated parts of James Joyce's *Ulysses* in "The Wasteland", but it could also be said that both T.S. Eliot and James Joyce had some of Dante Alghieri's *The Divine Comedy* going on too much in their own work. Alex Haley admitted that Roots contains whole passages lifted from Harold Courlander's 1967 novel, *The African*: `Somewhere somebody gave me something that came from The African. That's the best, honest explanation I can give.` Shin Kyung-sook, who won the 2011 Man Asia Literary Prize for the novel *Please Look After Mom*, has to deal with accusations of plagiarism upon almost every publication of a new short story collection or a new novel. She has been accused of over-emulating Mishima Yukio, Luise Rinser, and many others.

Worthy of the Event

She denies copying but does say, `Sometimes when I read novels, I find passages — sometimes the entire episode — that are in perfect sync with my own thoughts.`

  John Hughes's novel, *The Dogs*, was removed from the longlist of Australia's most important literary prize because some sentences appeared to have been lifted from oral testi-monies in the English translation of Svetlana Alexievich's *The Unwomanly Face of War*. As a writer, John Hughes has always been a great emulator. He writes right at the border of fictive and actual. He works so inspired by the work of others, he just has to do them, and he just has to try to do the others he admires better than they do themselves. John Hughes's main explanation for the apparently unoriginal material in *The Dogs* seemed to be, that is how I work, it's my writing process, and every writing process is, in practice, a kind of aemulatio, although he didn't use that particular word. A bevy of Australian literary tweeters fired up the Turnitin app and other algorithms on *The Dogs* for weeks. They must have liked the big increase in their likes on Twitter/X and they must have felt worthy of something, but not events, when all those self-righteous shocked comments flooded in after their ongoing work with Turnitin and various other algorithms revealed omg OMG similarities in the structure of *The Dogs* to works by W. G. Sebald, Leo Tolstoy, F. Scott Fitzgerald, Andrei Makine, Nadezhda Mandelstam, Erich Maria Remarque, and Jordan Peterson although not Eileen Myles, not Dodie Bellamy, not *me*.

•

Kanye West before he became Ye, before he became an anti-Semite, and before he accused Adidas of over-emulating the design of Yeezy Flip-Flops, tweets: `too much emphasis is put on originality. Feel free to take ideas and update them at your will all great artists take and update.`

•

On the third day of the third lunar month of the year 353, Wang Xizhi wrote "Preface to the Poems of the Orchid Pavilion" quickly and with friends after too much wine at the Orchid Pavilion on what is now Mount Xianglu in Zhejiang Province in eastern China. Since that tipsy evening, countless copies of "Preface to the Poems of the Orchid Pavilion" have been made. Ten thousand are being made at this very moment somewhere in some calligraphy and classical poetry classes, in calligraphy ateliers in Taiwan, the People's Republic of China, Singapore, Malaysia, Australia, and wherever Chinese diaspora is found, and nobody says with exclamation marks and seriously raised eyebrows: Plagiarism!! Zhao Mengfu remarked in the thirteenth century: `There is no way to know how many tens of hundreds of versions were made, and it began to be hard to tell apart the real and the fake.` Some of the copies of "Preface to the Poems of the Orchid Pavilion" are considered sublime in themselves, so beautiful and expert are they, they are held as great treasures in the Metropolitan Museum of Art, Tokyo National Museum, the British Museum, Musée Cernuschi, and other places where originality is customarily the most important arbiter of both artistic and monetary value.

Worthy of the Event

✳

V. S. Naipaul understood his own writing to be a kind of emulation of the literary forms and styles of the British writers taught at his very good school in the colony of Trinidad and Tobago. After the great success of *A House for Mr Biswas*, V. S. Naipaul visited India. He went to discover his ancestral homeland and found a lot of trouble there, poverty, and what V.S. Naipaul thought of as a kind of indolence, and especially Indians shitting in the open air, that is what is wrong with India, V.S. Naipaul reckoned, although almost everything else subcontinental repulsed him too. He was perpetually ready for fecal horror in India, and he found it: pools of runny yellow shit, well-formed turds being a privilege of wealth, and all the squatting, and bare arses or asses, and grunting and shitting in public turning India into an area of darkness, and all that public shitting in the Chennai bus station, on floors, in urinals and on patios, Indians defecate everywhere. They defecate, mostly, beside the railway tracks. But they also defecate on the beaches; they defecate on the hills; they defecate on the riverbanks; they defecate on the street; they never look for cover. Let them use toilets.

 I have read that six hundred and seventy-five million Indians still open their bowels wherever they think it best to open their bowels or wherever they *must* open their bowels because there is no better nor safer place for shitting.

Government fecal hygiene and toilet installation projects, of which there are many, mostly fail because who wants to do their business indoors when the new toilets are shit-strewn holes miles from home or too close to home when one can shit beneath the silver braids of stars or in the scorch of the noonday sun or in the sympathetic shade of a neem tree or even in a corner of the porch, or if you like to dislike the way things are going, one may take a dump along West Veli Street across from Madurai Station and leave your pool of ordure or your warm coils at the base of a wall covered in giant cinematic posters of Amma, who is running for Chief Minister of Tamil Nadu *again*, turds desiccating in the sun below a poster of the current prime minister, who seems to have a false beard and too much blusher applied to his decisive cheeks, and is that a halo? Hiding shit in India is a remnant of colonial power, some Indian scholars say, doing it in the open might be an act of resistance to the mistakes and cruelties of the post-colonial state, they say.

Public shitting in India, public shitting anywhere, might be one of James Scott's weapons of the weak, for shit exists in an intimate and honest relationship with the thinking and feelings of the shitter. Shit may be the real threat to order; Maria M. was right to say that shit and the anus have the power to fight back. The threat of shit is the threat of the remainder. Shit is the threat of bodily matter breaking the body limit. Shit is the threat posed to citizenship when part of the citizen's body leaves the body. Shit beyond the limit of the body is a stool pigeon pumping out antithetical intel against the rules about the body as a sacred temple, the body as the fortress of subjectivity, the body as limited to itself, the body of the state completed. The body of evidence becomes a body of lies when shit gets out, and the student body plagiarizing shit everywhere, the body corporate, bodies of water, this is not water, this is shit, this is me and *that* shit is not me, that essay about shit and shitting bears no resemblance to an essay, it is too personal, too much body, it is a heap of shit.

※

Dodie Bellamy says Eileen Myles says a good transition is the most important thing. I say she's right. I say a good transition bears the reader *from* any kind of shit *to* any kind of shit, easy and happy to go. I doubt my mother ever read anything Eileen Myles or Dodie Bellamy, and if my mother noticed a bad transition in any one of the two-a-week-for-seventy-three-years novels she read, she was unlikely to do more than snort and say, "That doesn't make sense." She did not need to elaborate in a literary way. Nor did she did need to be told to manage her final transition beautifully. My mother died so adroitly it was easy to accept she was dead when she was dead. She had death down like *that*. She was soooo worthy of it.

One of the last things I pull from the completely open ass/arse/anus of my car in the dump-your-shit-in-these bin parking lot by the shit-brown river is a black wool poncho threaded with silver yarn and fifteen black pom-poms jouncing from its hem, a gift from my mother last year, and I could not say no to it. Nor could I say, I see from this that you know nothing about me or know not enough about me to know that I wouldn't be seen dead within five miles of a pom-pom, though ponchos were back in back then, and black is always, and I could clip the pom-poms off, but the silver yarn threaded through the black wool, well, certainly not. It is not in me to send the black-with-silver-threads-and-fifteen-pom-poms poncho off to be dead white people's clothes in Ghana, so I put it back in the car and take it home again, and, eventually, pom-poms and all, I wear it for my mother the next time I visit. She hasn't had her morning oxycodone. She says, "Metallics in the morning?" and she says, "First, you had your face changed trying to copy something, that whatshername, Vanessa Redgrave, the tall one, weren't you, or something you've tried with your face, I'll never know, will I, and now you're doing blonde again. Who are you trying to be? Just be yourself, stop copycatting, that is good enough for me, I am your old mother."

I have not had my face changed. I don't look like Vanessa Redgrave, except the tall part. I look like my mother. She flows in me. I have watched her forever. I've practiced parts of my mother so that I can perfect in *parts of me* the way she is with autonomy, always show your cheekbones, throw your head back when you laugh, not *that* far or your head will fall off, and how to be aspirational about alone. Parts of my mother come out of me like parts of Joni Mitchell come out of Prince in his cover version of "A Case of You."

"You had your front teeth crowned at the age of ninety," I say to my mother. "Who were you trying to be then?"

She gives me one of her anymore-of-that-and-you'll-get-the-rough-edge-of-my-tongue-or-something-worse looks, and she says, "These crowns were a medical necessity sort of thing. That awful nurse is late with my pill again. She thinks she's the Queen of Fiji or somewhere, that one, she does."

Next winter and my mother is dying. She is almost beyond giving and receiving. Next winter my mother twists and arches herself in bed when I come to her. Her eyes shut; her fingers busy. Her fingers *scrabble*, that is what my mother's fingers do, but they scrabble at nothing or against the fall into nothing, who knows. "Help me, oh, help me, help me, oh, please, help me," my mother says. The `awful Queen of Fiji` nurse comes in soft and kind and gives my mother a shot of morphine or something else strong and lovely, and after five minutes of more struggling and pleading with ectoplasmic interlocutors, my mother settles down. She opens her eyes , formerly olive-green with carnelian flecks but gone the hard and washed-out grey of river stones now my mother's eyes, and her pupils intensely miotic, withered down to black specks by the drug or by organ failure or by what she sees coming just for her, here it is, my mother's personal black star.

She is there but not here. She is my mother and not quite my mother. We spend our last day together here there but not there until the light turns long and coppery and the white cockatoos start shrieking about cold night coming. "Oh, I'm pooing," my mother says. "Oh, dear, oh dear, where's the lavatory, I'm going, it's coming now, I'm pooing. Oh, stop it."

I can't stop it. I can't find a bedpan, so I make a cushion of toilet paper, and I roll the bed covers down and I roll her nightgown up until my mother's legs appear and that tight skin on her shins shining mauve in the hospital light, and higher, I roll, until my mother's bottom appears, quite flawless and untouched by ninety-three years of sitting, shitting, and whatever else bottoms get up to. "Oh, oh, no, here it comes. Stop it," she says, and soon, after a minute of yotto yotto effort, she's making the effort, a long banana of shit, dark and smelling of iron, slips from my mother's arse onto the wad of toilet paper. "Oh, I'm dirty, dirty, dirty, disgusting," she says. "I'm filthy."

I dump her brooding and metallic stool in the lavatory. I run warm water into a blue pan. I moisten a white towel and soften up some lavender soap. My mother chants: "No no no no no no. No no no no no no. No no no no no no no no. Nooooooo. Stop it."

I don't care about no. No is not me now. I am all yes. Don't ask me to stop anything. I care about wash and wipe. I care about not seeing too much more *up there*. I care about a clean nightgown and a dust of lavender talcum powder and lavender cream on her hands and face, pat, pat, Mum/Mom/Mother/oh, Mummy, don't go.

"It hurts," she says.

That `Queen of Fiji awful` nurse comes with another tender injection of something lovely and my mother goes off again, stuporous and still, she goes, except for her mouth which will not stop. She tells stories not much longer than flickers: light hurt me; I said no; fish for tea. She says hello to people I never knew. She gasps; she

Worthy of the Event

sighs. She makes sympathetic clucks and tsks about some tale of woe, some disgraceful conduct. There is a bout of tears luxuriant and falling. "Oh, you you you you you you," she says, but my mother's tears and her you you you you are not about me, not about shitting herself. She does not shed tears about the closing of some existential loop begun with cleaning up *my* baby shit and now completing itself at last with me cleaning up *her* mother shit, she doesn't weep about *that*, there at the lip of the event horizon, not my mother; *her* tears are for something else, someone else, some shame, some memory, some story I have never heard, some much earlier paragraph she is in as she dies, "I'm sorry, I'm sorry, I'm sorry." More tears. "I couldn't do anything else, it would have killed Mum and Dad, the baby, after Snow. Oh dear, what could I do."

My mother's body at the end and its adieu shitting dismantle all my stories about my mother and me and there is no Georges Bataille nor any Julia Kristeva in it. My mother's final shit makes me tender when I have never been tender about my mother before, and, no, you may not think my tender at the last minute is too late for tender; it is not too late for tenderness for my tender is the kind of tender that lasts forever, unending tender now. I am so tender. I am myself. I bend over my mother and find her long ear all pleated by years of disappointing tidings, and I whisper into it, `I'm going to kiss you and when you fall asleep, I'll stab you like a knife.`

She gets a Mona Lisa kind of smile, and we hold hands for hours until I say, "I am going now. I will come back, but don't wait for me, you don't have to wait for me," because *you don't have to wait for me* is something I have read you might want to say to a dying person.

My mother sits up. She fixes me with those eyes-not-really-my-mother's eyes and she says with great conviction, "I will be waiting for you, I will wait for you, I will be waiting in the garden and the magnolia is flowering, oh, you never seen anything like it, see, look, look, the wattle trees are like gold by the river, the birds are having a party in it, and the new leaves on the Japanese maple are so green it almost hurts my eyes, oh my eyes, I can see you, and I will be waiting in the garden for you and when you come, when you come, come soon, come later, when you do come, everything that is wrong will be right again, it will be perfect."

```
Body, scatter in the dust of the sky.
```

Acknowledgements

All who gave: Kristen Keegan Ingalz and Trish Falvo were especially generous when I needed funds to continue with the early development of the project that resulted in this book, which is almost certainly not the book you expected from me, but it is yours, anyway. Lucca Fraser gave abundantly of her time and her critical abilities to read several drafts of every chapter. joanne burns made a suggestion that sent me from the book I thought I had to this book. I am not entirely sure, but I think Jackie Ess arranged publication in *The Believer* of what became the sixth chapter. The buzz of publishing there gave me the energy to do the rest. Kaya Wilson was endlessly enthusiastic and encouraging throughout. Robyn Graf took me out to lunches and coffee and read everything and said it was fabulous. Jonathan Dunk (*Overland Literary Journal*) said, "Are you doing a book? You should." Casey Plett and Cat Fitzpatrick (LittlePuss Press) are the best publisher and editor (respectively) in the whole wide world.

Earlier versions of the disappointments and the disappearance of a.k.a. Victor Mature were published at *Overland Literary Journal*. A previous version of stardust was published at *The Believer* as "La Folía" and a slightly different draft of nuclear cats appeared in *Meanjin* along with the works of three other finalists for the 2021 Melbourne Prize for Literature.

About the Author

Vivian Blaxell currently lives in Naarm/Melbourne.

About LittlePuss Press

LittlePuss Press is a feminist press run by trans women. We believe in intensive editing, printing on paper, and throwing lots of parties.

A Note on the Type

This book is set in Adobe Caslon, a revival typeface based on the work on William Caslon (1692-1766) and designed by Carol Twombly in 1990. A few years after designing this face, Twombly abruptly abandoned her extremely successful career as a type designer. She now lives quietly in a small community in the Sierra foothills, practicing Qi Gong and Afrocuban drumming, hiking, volunteering locally.

The quotations are set in Prestige Elite, a typeface designed by Howard Kettler in 1953 for use on IBM type-writers. It is effective in materials for personal communication or for capturing the look and feel of bygone days.